TO
JOHN,

BE UNSTOPPABLE. o

2022

UNSTOPPABLE!

Inspiring Lessons for the Unstoppable You!

G. CRAIG CONRAD

LIFETIME CHRONICLE PRESS

Montrose, CO

Library of Congress Control Number: 2008921825

ISBN-13: 978-0-9814539-0-3

Second Edition, 2015
Fifth Printing, 2018
Printed in Canada

Cover design by Matt Beckett
Photos courtesy of Tracy Spencer of Lifetime Photography,
www.LifetimePhotoStudio.com

Published by:
Lifetime Chronicle Press
121 N. Park Ave.
Montrose, CO 81401
970-240-1345
chronicle@montrose.net

DEDICATION

This book is dedicated to my wife, **Vicki**. You have been my inspiration. This book would never have been published without all of your unselfish efforts. You have stood by my side for more than twenty-six years, and I realize now more than ever, the two smartest words I ever said was "I do."

To my son **Colton**. May you continue to have the strength and courage to live your own life. You are destined to become a man amongst men.

ACKNOWLEDGMENTS

To my parents, **George and Delores Conrad**, for instilling the morals and character that became the foundation on which I was able to build a successful teaching career.

A very special heartfelt thanks to **Ned** for his unwavering and enthusiastic support and unbelievable commitment in assisting me to spread *The Unstoppable You* message. Not only have you made my dream come true, but also the dreams of many others who will find the inspiration within these pages to become UNSTOPPABLE!

To my trusted friend and colleague, **Lance Scranton**, who helped show me *the way*.

To **Katy Gray**, thanks for your assistance and support.

To the **thousands of students** I've had the privilege of teaching for twenty-six years. Hopefully you learned as much from me as I did from you! Thanks.

And finally, thank **you** for buying this book. A portion of the proceeds from the sale of this book will go to charity.

PREFACE

The overwhelming majority of the stories you are about to read occurred during the span of my twenty-six year teaching career, with several dating back to my childhood. I did my best to recall the actual names and events in each story.

Amazingly, I was able to track down close to one hundred people and received permission to use their real names. Initially, this proved to be a daunting task. However, it was delightfully rewarding reconnecting with former students who are literally spread across the globe. Without exception, they said it was an honor to be included in the book, including two who are in prison. I was unable to locate just a few, and I only used their first name, or in one case, a fictitious name. Sadly, the story *Second Hour Class* is about one of my students who made the ultimate sacrifice while serving our country. I use his real name as a tribute to all who have served and continue to serve our great nation.

THE LESSON PLAN
(TABLE OF CONTENTS)

INTRODUCTION

"WE ARE DESIGNED FOR SUCCESS — BUT TOO OFTEN — PROGRAMMED FOR FAILURE."

Craig Conrad has the stories to prove that everyone has the capacity to succeed beyond their own "programmed" expectations. *The Unstoppable You* program has been the passionate, driving force behind the true stories you are about to read. One thing must be made clear from the outset: as you read this book, be prepared to be caught up in an amazing, truthful account of the influence of one man's tireless pledge to impact the lives of everyone around him.

I met Craig over ten years ago when I came to teach and coach at the same high school where Craig has built one of the most successful Woods program in the country. His "Woodshop" class has been recognized nationally as "A Classroom of Excellence." Craig has also been recognized and received the Governor's Award for Excellence in Education presented to him by the Governor of Colorado.

However, Craig will tell you (using a story, of course) that recognition is simply the result of him having the privilege to report the successes of those who have been a part of his own UNSTOPPABLE story over the past twenty-six years. Stories that celebrate the willingness of people around him to "Believe in the Power Within." Students in Craig's Woodshop classes are clearly moved by the stories he relates each Friday. Craig has moved from reading stories to recounting the true-life experiences of his students who have become, "The Friday Story." Students look forward to hearing about how other students have been impacted by the UNSTOPPABLE message, however, Craig is forthright and honest as he makes clear the consequence of those who do not heed the lessons learned in Craig's classroom.

I have witnessed Craig's passion for people — in the classroom as a teacher, in the community as a citizen, and at the national level as a speaker. Craig frequently presents *The Unstoppable You* to high schools, colleges, and at conferences all over the country. His personality draws you in, his approach causes you to take notice, and his powerful presentation of real stories, about real people, and real experiences, drives home the UNSTOPPA-BLE message.

If you already haven't figured it out — Craig MOTIVATES people of all ages to become something better than average in a world where he often exclaims that too many people are "striving to be average." Craig refuses to allow students or his audiences to accept the fate of those who simply live for the moment, who don't think that their decisions today will affect their tomorrow.

Incorporating his own brand of humor, mixed with the seriousness of the message, Craig has the gifted ability to make these stories real to the audience so that his message is clear. In *UNSTOPPABLE!* he presents to his audience the life-altering choices of real people and the impact of their decisions, which moderate from being sentenced to life in prison, to running without legs, to making the ultimate sacrifice as a soldier in service to our country.

We all need someone who will remind us of the greatness within each of us to do things that we might never have thought possible; a person to show us the power we have within ourselves to make decisions that will positively impact our future; and a person who will stand in front of us and encourage us to do better and that the days ahead are filled with the blessings of opportunity based on the choices we make.

The stories that make up this book, *UNSTOPPABLE!*, are the culmination of one man's conviction that one person can make a difference. People all over this country have been impacted by Craig's unwavering commitment to the power within each of us to live, as we should — UNSTOPPABLE!

I have often wished that Craig's stories were available to kids and adults to read for themselves, and to share with others, the powerful UNSTOPPABLE message. Thanks to Craig's willingness to sit down over the past year and a half and put his stories to paper, we now have the opportunity to read the stories, sharing in the excitement, and acknowledge that the experiences of others are often our best teacher.

— Lance Scranton

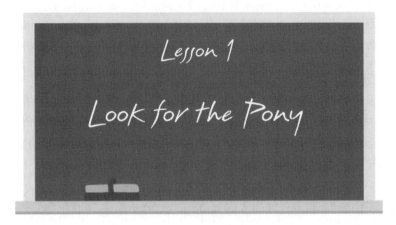

Lesson 1

Look for the Pony

I CAN NO LONGER RECALL what my brother Kevin and I were fighting about that day long ago, but I'll never forget Dad's advice. "Look for the pony," he said to me, when once again I complained about my brother.

I didn't realize then that Dad's words of wisdom would change my life forever almost twenty years later, not to mention the impact those words would have on tens of thousands of others...

Actually, Dad didn't say, "Look for the pony," at first. He simply asked me if I knew what an optimist was. I gave the most intelligent answer any second grader could muster. "Isn't he the guy that fixes your glasses?" I asked inquisitively.

When Dad finished laughing, he told me an optimist always looks at the bright or positive side to all of life's situations, while a pessimist always looks at the dark or negative side. Sensing my confusion, he told me this Christmas story...

The story was about two brothers who raced downstairs Christmas morning to discover their presents underneath the tree. Upon opening his first gift, the pessimistic brother found a beautiful, red, shiny fire truck. Almost instantly, he started complaining about the present, eventually tossing it to the side. On the other hand, the optimistic brother smiled joyfully after discovering a single piece of horse poop in his first box.

The pessimistic brother snarled after opening his second gift. It was a beautiful brown, leather baseball glove but he had asked Santa for a tan one. Meanwhile, his optimistic brother was giggling and laughing after discovering his second box was filled with more horse poop.

The pessimist threw a tantrum after opening the box with a sparkling new Tonka Toy, because it wasn't the exact one he wanted. The optimist could hardly wait to open his last present, the biggest box of all! When he tore off the lid, he couldn't believe his eyes! It was filled to the brim with more horse poop! The optimist started screaming and yelling, jumping up and down. That's when the pessimistic brother asked, "Are you crazy? You just got three boxes of horse poop! What in the world could you possibly be so excited about?"

To which the optimistic brother exclaimed, "With all of this horse poop, there's gotta be a pony around here somewhere!"

Dad's message was, "Son, look for the pony." Now, I must confess, that, as a second grader, I truly didn't understand the significance of his message, but opening Christmas gifts later that year had a whole new twist of excitement and anticipation.

Twenty years later, I would desperately need to recall that story as a wood shop teacher up to my neck in poop, so to speak. Eventually I was able to find the pony, but only after I was told, ***"You're fired..."***

The Unstoppable You must look for the pony
in any situation, and when you find that pony,
ride 'em for all it's worth!

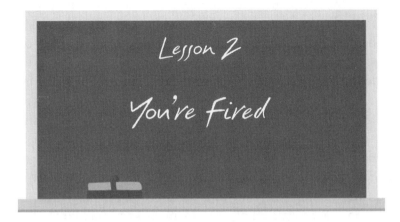

Lesson 2

You're Fired

"YOU'RE FIRED!" Never in my life did I think I would hear those words, much less hear them on the radio. But, that's how I unofficially heard I had been RIFed (reduction in force) in 1985. A huge drop in enrollment due to the completion of a local power plant left a fellow teacher with too few students so, the district cut his program. Since he was tenured, and I was the new kid on the block, he was given my job. I was left unemployed after just recently getting married, selling my old business, and moving 2,000 miles from home. To add insult to injury, as I already mentioned, I first heard about it on the local radio before I was officially given my pink slip — and it actually was *pink*! Losing your job is hard enough, but losing your job because someone else didn't have enough kids in his class — that's just unbelievable!

But, looking back on it now, it was one of the best things that has ever happened to me. As the saying goes, things work out best for those who make the best of the way things work out. I worked as the district maintenance man for a half-year, plowing snow, hanging drywall, assisting the plumber and electrician, and generally feeling sorry for myself — until it hit me one day. "You're getting paid to learn these different trades." And that changed everything.

At that same time, many of the people in our town who had built the power plant could not sell their homes. When they left town, the banks repossessed their homes, and I purchased several of them, using my maintenance skills to renovate them. I resold those homes at a much larger profit than the salary I would have made teaching. At the time, it was the biggest risk I had ever taken.

After one year, the teacher who took over my job was asked to leave, and I got my teaching position back thanks to Dr. Charles Grove, the superintendent. However, the situation was dark and about to get darker. My old shop had fallen victim to pilferage and vandalism; the budget was thousands in the red; and enrollment had dwindled to the point that the job became part-time. I was given one year to turn it all around, or, as I was told by Dr. Grove, "We'll have to shut it down." As if that wasn't bad enough, at no time did they tell me Levi would be in my class, and that would lead to my darkest hour. But, **when it's darkest, that's when the stars come out...**

The Unstoppable You knows that things work out best for those who make the best of the way things work out.

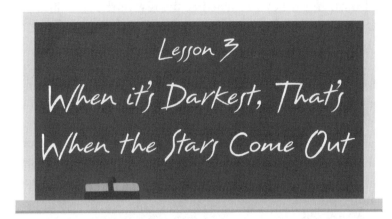

Lesson 3

When it's Darkest, That's When the Stars Come Out

PERHAPS I OWE LEVI a large dose of gratitude. After all, he single-handedly forced me to change the way I teach forever. I've told this story to tens of thousands. Funny, on the day I exploded, I didn't see it that way. It was just Levi doing what he did best... being a pain in my "class."

I was given a ride back to work after dropping off a school van that day. As we approached the building, I saw Levi standing boldly in front of the school, smoking pot. You might say he was taking his own "class trip." I jumped out of the van and hauled him to the office, where he lied and denied it all. Later that same morning in my class, Levi walked by me and said, "Thought you got me," while laughing. I was at the breaking point. I grabbed him by the shirt and laid him on the work table. I had my nose one inch away from his, and I was screaming at the top of my lungs. Specks of spittle rained down on Levi's face.

I have said it for years, that those in the teaching profession are thirty seconds from losing their job each day. How? Some kid pushes your buttons on a bad day and refuses to stop, and you lose it. What you do in those next thirty seconds could determine the rest of your future. Well, on this day, I was literally about ten seconds away from slugging a major attitude adjustment on my "favorite" student. Luckily for Levi, he didn't smart off at that moment, because if he would have said anything — even help

— this story would have a whole different ending. When I finished shouting at Levi, I turned to the rest of the class and yelled, "The rest of you, get busy!" Boy, they got busy. I scared them all! But when they left that day, I couldn't help but think Levi was the hero. He caused me to lose it. I pictured kids coming up to him and congratulating him, saying, "Dude, that was cool. Glad it wasn't me. Did you see that vein ready to pop out of Conrad's head?"

That was the exact moment I remembered Dad's story of twenty years ago. "Son, look for the pony." I realized there had to be a pony around here somewhere, 'cause I was up to my neck in the horse poop!

What I decided to do was give the kids something positive every Friday. Back then, I called it the thought for the weekend. One Friday, while they were lined up to leave, I told them, "When it's darkest, that's when the stars come out."

Most of them laughed and said, "So does the moon." Some looked dazed and confused. Come to think of it, that's how they always looked. There was one kid, Dale Musgrave, who got it. You could see the lightbulb come on. The others didn't have a clue.
When I played basketball in high school, *I* led the league in scoring, not just my team. But during one crucial game, I went down right before halftime with what was thought to be a sprained ankle. Knowing I needed to play if the team was to have a chance of winning, coach pointed right at me in front of everyone and said, "Son, when it's darkest, that's when the stars come out!"
I played the second half. After the game, I was told the ankle was separated. We lost the game, but I never lost the saying. That saying would become a belief. That belief would later become a conviction that would not only change my life, but Dale Musgrave's as well.

Dale was a wrestler on our high school wrestling team, so talented that he qualified for state. However, the week before state, Dale broke his hand at practice, ruining his chance to compete for the championship. He went home that night with his hand in a cast and his arm in a sling, and his father told him that the guy he beat at districts would take his place at state. CHSAA rules prohibit anyone from wrestling with a cast on their arm. That night, in his living room, Dale held his cast up in the air and told his dad, "When it's darkest, that's when the stars come out!"

All week long at school, classmates, teachers, and teammates said, "Tough break" — literally — "but you've got nothing to be ashamed of." To everyone, Dale's reply was, "When it's darkest, that's when the stars come out." Those words became his power from within, and the power from within is Unstoppable!

Because he earned the right to go to state, our school allowed him to travel the 250 miles to Denver, even though he couldn't compete, but Dale had another plan. After the excitement of the opening ceremony, he turned to his coach, Roman Gutierrez, and said, "Cut the cast off. I didn't come to watch; I came to wrestle!" Instead of feeling sorry for himself, Dale was looking for the pony. Dale's pony would be the power from within, and the belief that his one good arm would beat all of the other wrestlers with two.

In that hour of darkness, a star was about to come out and would shine so brilliantly that it would light up the entire arena. On that weekend, Dale didn't just wrestle, he won the state championship, with a broken hand! Afterward, he could not even hold up the cardboard bracket of his championship matches. They recast his hand immediately. Coach Roman Gutierrez would eventually go on to win five state championship team titles, ensuring his spot in the Hall of Fame as one of the greatest high school wrestling coaches in Colorado.

When Dale got back to class on Monday, he stuck his good hand out at me. At first, being a wood shop teacher, I thought he cut himself. "What's the matter?" I asked.

"Nothing," Dale said. "I just want to shake your hand."

"Why?" I asked.

"Because, I just won the state championship, and I wanted to let you know you were a big part of it."

"How was I a big part of it?" I questioned. "I didn't teach you any moves or techniques."

"No, what you taught me is that no matter how dark it gets, my star can still shine. Thanks man!"

I'll never forget what I did next. I walked up to my desk, opened the drawer, and pulled out a letter that I had worked on for a long time. I read the words on the letter that day and thought about all the problems with my program and job, and what had just happened with Dale. Then I took that letter, tore it up, and threw it in the trash. What I threw in the trash that day was my letter of resignation. Back when I first told Dale's class "When it's darkest..." and they all laughed and made fun, I figured the heck with this. I don't need this job and the hassles. Thank God, Dale helped me to find the pony. Along with that, I would need to learn to **break the chains...**

The Unstoppable You lives for when it's darkest...
because that's when you shine the brightest.
Shine on, shining star!

Lesson 4

Break the Chains

I WAS PUMPED THE FIRST TIME the circus came to our little town in northwest Colorado. I couldn't wait to take our two-year-old son, Colton. He had never been to the circus before. Well, at least that was my excuse for going. Fact was, I had never been to the circus before, either. What we saw there was entertaining, but what I *learned* at the circus was empowering and unforgettable!

This traveling circus was billed as having twenty elephants, more than any other. Sure enough, after the majority of the acts were over, in came the elephants, the highlight of the show! They marched around the ring and stopped right in front of us. Then they got up on their hind legs and turned toward us. Now, we were sitting in the front row, and I'm looking up at this foot the size of a desk — trying to show no fear to my two year old, and thinking, "I hope that elephant doesn't lose his balance!" Meanwhile, Colton was giggling and pointing, saying, "Daddy, elephant...Daddy, elephant!" The elephants did a few more tricks, then they left. They did all of this with one guy tapping the elephant with a stick.

I was impressed, until I went outside and saw all twenty elephants just standing there. I was amazed! Kids were crawling all over them. Every one of those elephants was held to the ground with a small stake and a little chain no bigger than what you would tie a dog with. When relating this story to my class, I asked, "Why were those elephants just standing there?"

One kid said, "They're in our town, and there's nothing better to do." I disagreed. If I were an elephant, I'd want to bust through the jungle, chasing girl elephants.

So, I questioned the guy with the stick. "How do you get them to do that?"

He said two words that I've never forgotten: "Learned helplessness." I asked him to explain. He proceeded to tell me how they conditioned the biggest and strongest animal, who walks the planet earth, to just stand there.

"We take 'em when they're a baby, 'cause even a baby elephant's really strong. We take a big, huge stake and pound it deep into the ground. Then we attach a thick, strong chain to the stake. Next, we bring Momma over. You see, Momma's been through the process, and baby follows. Now we chain baby to the stake, and take Momma away. Baby cries out for Momma, 'Momma!' Momma cries back, 'Baby, come here, come here!' Pulling with all of its might, baby cries, 'I can't, I can't, I can't.' This goes on for several days until the baby elephant's self talk goes from, 'I can't, I can't,' to 'I won't, I won't,' to 'I don't, I don't.' Then you don't need such a big stake, or a thick chain. You can get the biggest and strongest animal that walks on the planet to just stand there. Because he does not think he can break the chain. There have been documented cases where elephants burned to death while chained to a stake, all the while believing they could not break the chains."

I looked into the eyes of those elephants at the circus. Do you think I saw a wild raging beast? No, I saw a depressed, defeated animal that had learned to be helpless. The really sad thing is, during my twenty-six years in the teaching profession, I've seen tons of kids who were just like those elephants, and a lot of teachers, too. People who were told so many times, "You can't, you can't," that gradually they became Stoppable! They don't. They don't. Here's a fact, my friend: you can either break the chains, or the chains are going to break you.

The first day Donnie walked into my classroom, it was plain to see those chains had been holding him down for years. I didn't realize that one day I would play a small role in helping Donnie break those chains. Over 700 people got to witness it that day in the auditorium. There wasn't a dry eye in the place. Even the toughest kids in the school were emotional watching Donnie on stage, as he showed them and told them to *fill your cup...*

The Unstoppable You knows you can either break the chains or the chains are going to break you.

Lesson 5

Fill Your Cup

I'M A TEACHER. My job is to teach the students. However, when I'm really lucky, I have students who teach me.

One of those students was Donnie McLeslie. Donnie taught me the world's biggest lie: all men are created equal. First of all, we're not all men, are we? Second, we're not all equal. Each one of us is unique and different. Fortunately, we live in a country that strives to provide the equal right to be unequal by choice. Even identical twins I taught through the years were different, at least on the inside.

What I learned from Dr. Denis Waitley and witnessed from Donnie is we all have a "cup." Your cup is your genetic makeup. It's all those things about yourself you can't change — your sex, your height, and your skin color. You can't change those...unless, of course, you're Michael Jackson! You got what you got. Some of you were blessed, and have huge cups: you're intelligent, strong, fast, and good looking. Others of us, like Donnie — well, let's just say our cups are not as big. The good news is, as was taught to me by Donnie, it's not the size of your cup that's important; it's how you fill it!

I think it's safe to say that in many ways, Donnie didn't even have a cup. He had more like a saucer. When he was a small child, a doctor misdiagnosed Donnie as severely mentally retarded. When he got to high school, they put him in my class, Woodworking.

One day my phone rang, and I was told Donnie would be enrolled in my class. Because I knew who he was, I questioned, "Why would you put a kid like that in a Woodworking class, considering the risk for injury?"

Then I was told, "Donnie can't read, so if there's anything of importance he needs to know, you need to read it to him."

As I hung up the phone, I resented the fact that they would put a kid like that in my woodworking class. "How stupid is that?" I remembered thinking. Now I know that I was the stupid one. In a normal situation, the teacher teaches the student. I would soon learn that Donnie was about to become *my* teacher.

Over the next few days and weeks, I read Donnie our safety tests after school. I got to really liking him because of his warm, friendly personality. Then, over the next few months, I started to learn from him. Here was a kid who didn't have half the size cup as the other kids in his class, but he filled it everyday. Many times, Donnie would sand a piece of wood until it literally shined. He would often leave class covered in sawdust. Laughing to himself as he left, he'd wave at me and say, "See ya morrow!"

Donnie finished all the required projects that year and made a spice rack for his mom as a final project. That spice rack never would have won a blue ribbon at our annual woodworking show. The drawers didn't open smoothly, and it was a little out of square. But that didn't matter. Donnie put a lot of love, time, and hard work into that spice rack, surprising his mom with it when he finished. She thought it was the best spice rack she had ever seen. "Best in the world," Donnie told me.

I couldn't help wondering if Donnie's classmates were blind. Did they not see what just occurred here? Here was a kid with half the size cup they had, finishing his project. Some of them, the big cups, didn't even get their projects completed. They failed the class! They should have been embarrassed to have worked alongside Donnie, who filled his cup everyday, in every way.

Donnie was also a wrestler, but his cup wasn't big enough to be on varsity. So, even in his senior year, Donnie was on junior varsity. One day, he invited me to come to his one and only home match. I told him, "You bet buddy; I'll be there for you."

I arrived early and waited through all the other matches, until the junior varsity heavyweight match. Donnie ran onto the mat, stripped off his sweat suit, and began warming up. This was going to be his one and only moment to shine. Donnie didn't have a clue what was about to occur. The other team didn't have a junior varsity heavyweight, so there was poor old Donnie, all dressed up and no place to go. He shrugged his shoulders at me with his head hung low as he walked off the mat. I shrugged my shoulders at him as if to say, "Sorry, Donnie, but there's nothing you can do about it." I leaned to my wife and whispered, "Gee, I wish there was something I could do."

Many people say everything happens for a reason, but I never really gave it much thought until I was about to witness it for myself later that night. Perhaps those people are right — maybe everything *does* happen for a reason.

I don't remember why I stayed to watch the varsity matches. I only went to see Donnie that night, and there were plenty of other things I needed to be doing. Whatever the reason, I stayed. I thank God I did! Had I left, I would have missed the greatest moment that ever took place in our gymnasium during my twenty-six years of teaching.

When the time came for the varsity heavyweight match, our guy was disqualified. The coach decided to substitute Donnie. It was only an exhibition match, since we had already forfeited the match due to the disqualification. Everyone could see the contest was a mismatch. The other guy's cup was huge! He was bigger, stronger, and he had a lot more moves than old "one move" Donnie... Wrestle!

It became quickly evident just how big the other guy's cup was. He was scoring points at will, taking Donnie down each time. But, every time Donnie went down, he got back up and did his one and only move. Late in the final period, it was obvious this was a huge mistake. Donnie hadn't scored a point and he was getting annihilated! But, this was an exhibition match, so they let it go. I turned to my wife with thirteen seconds to go and said, "This is the worst thing that could have happened to Donnie. He would have been better off if he hadn't wrestled tonight."

And that's when it happened. I don't know why, but I think Mr. Big Cup looked up at the scoreboard, and decided to stop filling his cup. With thirteen seconds to go, Donnie got his one and only move around that guy's neck. Our gymnasium erupted with cheers! With eight seconds to go, Donnie took him down on the mat — and as if on cue — everyone in the gym stood on their feet. With four seconds left in the match, Donnie pinned him! Donnie won! Tears streamed down both my cheeks that night as I got to witness first hand, *It's not the size of your cup that's important, it's how you fill it.* I'll tell you something else, two cups runneth over that night. Donnie's and mine.

I jumped from the bleachers and ran down to the mat to congratulate Donnie and say thank-you... But that, as they say, is **the best part of the story...**

The Unstoppable You knows it's not the size of your cup that's important...it's how you fill it.

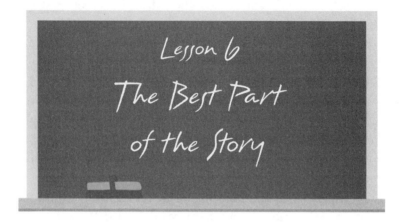

Lesson 6
The Best Part
of the Story

AFTER DONNIE WON HIS WRESTLING MATCH, I truly wanted to thank him. He taught all of us an unforgettable lesson that night. Knowing Donnie was the world's biggest Denver Bronco fan, I asked him if he wanted to watch them that Sunday.

At first, Donnie said, "I'll be over," thinking I was inviting him over to my house where, together, we watched many of the Bronco games.

"No, Donnie, you're not coming over to my house this Sunday. How would you like to go see the Bronco's live and in person?" I asked.

For the first time since I've known him, Donnie was speechless. He just kept nodding his head...

Yes.

Yes.

Yes.

Next, I had to round up some tickets; no easy feat in Colorado. Thanks to the help of another teacher who was also inspired that day, we rounded up three tickets.

That Sunday, before we jumped in the car, Donnie and I made our weekly bet on the winner of the game. Donnie, of course, would always choose the Broncos. Just to fire him up, I would always take their opponent. This week that was the Indianapolis Colts.

Since we were actually going to the game, I told Donnie, "We have to have a special bet." We agreed that should the Broncos win, I would walk home. If the Broncos lost, Donnie would do the walking. Donnie had never been to Denver before, so he didn't realize the walk home was over 250 miles. It didn't matter, the bet was just for fun, and Donnie wasn't thinking about going home. He was too excited to get to Mile High Stadium.

We arrived in Denver an hour early. My wife, Vicki, took advantage of that extra hour by doing what she loves best. Shopping!

As Donnie and I walked through the mall, he asked, "What's that?"

"That's an escalator, Donnie."

"What do?"

"It takes you up to the second floor," I told him.

"Let's go," he said. So, we rode the escalator up and down several times that afternoon. Donnie got such a kick out of walking without walking, riding that escalator for the first time. He laughed the whole time!

As for myself, I was filled with anxiety knowing that Vicki had been recently diagnosed with "the field of dreams shopping syndrome."

"What's that?" I asked the doctor.

The doctor told me that she hears this little voice inside of her head that whispers, "If you spend it, more will come." Ha,ha!

When we finally arrived at Mile High Stadium and Donnie walked through the cold cement corridors, he had no clue that what he watched each Sunday on television would look so much bigger and better in person. When he stepped through the corridor and out into the stadium, he just stood there and stared in disbelief.

Paratroopers jumped from an an airplane streaming orange and blue smoke! The Denver Broncos ran out onto the field. The crowd was electric! The noise was incredible, off the charts! I thought I saw Donnie pinching himself!

This was John Elway's first year as Denver's pro quarterback. Everyone had high expectations since the Broncos had paid millions for him. However, John hadn't proven his worth to this point. The game before this, they had beaten a playoff team, and the fans were sure their "million dollar man" had arrived. The Colts, on the other hand, had not won a game. This one was going to be a blowout!

Sure enough, at the end of the third quarter, the score was 19-0, Broncos...losing! Amazingly, just like Donnie's wrestling match!

The fans were booing the Broncos. They chanted, "No way, Elway. Kubiak, Kubiak," chanting for the back-up quarterback, Gary Kubiak.

Donnie turned to me at the start of the fourth quarter, visibly upset and crying. I thought he was crying because the fans were booing his Broncos and yelling, "No way, Elway!"

The only thing Donnie said was, "You make me walk?" The poor guy was worried about walking home!

I really felt bad for Donnie, and at a loss for words I told him, "A deal is a deal, and a bet is a bet." He started crying more! "Come on, Broncos — at least score a touchdown," I was thinking to myself. Donnie hadn't gotten to cheer since the opening introductions.

Elway threw a touchdown at the start of the fourth quarter, making the score 7-19, but the fans still called for Kubiak. Halfway through the fourth quarter, the defense intercepted a pass and ran it back for a score, 14-19. That's when we both experienced that Rocky Mountain thunder at Mile Hi Stadium. I was moving, but I wasn't moving. The stadium was shaking!

With less than two minutes left in the game, Elway found Gerald Willhite in the end zone. Touchdown! The Broncos won 21-19! Pandemonium ensued afterwards. People were going nuts pushing, yelling, and screaming, "Broncos, Broncos!"

Even on the bus ride back to where we had parked the car, it was crazy! Donnie was like a sponge. He was soaking it all in.

I thanked God. I couldn't have written a better script to the ending of the game. It was just like Donnie's wrestling match, don't quit, never give up, fill your cup! It was just like how he lived his life.

But I knew what was coming. Donnie was smart: he didn't say a word until after we went out for dinner. Not until after he had finished his meal, that I had paid for, did he mention our bet. "A deal is a deal, a bet is a bet," he reminded me.

"Yeah, but Donnie...ah humina, ah humina," I stammered.

Then Donnie used a saying against me that I had taught him. I hate it when that happens! He said, "Are you a man of your word, or simply the words of a man?"

Ouch, that hurt! "You're right, Donnie. I'm walking home," I said. "But I'm taking the car keys with me, unless we strike a deal where I can chauffeur you back to town." Needless to say, we struck a deal.

I'm embarrassed to say that Donnie graduated from high school unable to read. I believe if you tell a kid he can't do something — or worse, that he believes he can't do something — then he won't he won't...he don't. It goes back to Lesson #4, Break the Chains. Those chains held Donnie down his whole life.

Until one night after graduating from high school. Donnie was washing dishes at the Holiday Inn when it hit him. "I don't want to do this anymore," he thought to himself. Just one problem stood in his way of getting another job: he couldn't read a job application. So now, for the first time in his life, Donnie understood the importance of learning to read.

He enrolled himself at CNCC, our local community college, to learn how to read. Before he signed up he asked me, "What do you think? You think I learn to read?"

I said, "Of course I do, Donnie, but what's really important is, what do you think?"

"I learn to read," is all he said.

Eventually, Donnie mastered reading so well — "hooked on phonics" you might say — that the time had come for what many students at our school said was the most awesome thing they had ever witnessed.

At an all school assembly — at the very school he graduated from, unable to read — I told Donnie's story, Fill Your Cup, to the crowd. I told them of all the obstacles Donnie had to overcome — including the recent death of his mother, the mom he had made the spice rack for. I told them how, dying from cancer, she no longer recognized Donnie and how he said he wished he would have told her he loved her more.

I told them about the two kids Donnie's sister had left with Donnie's mother to raise, and how Donnie was now left with the task of raising two kids. I ended by telling how Donnie wanted to be a teacher, but he didn't know how to get the degree.

"Ladies and gentlemen," I proudly proclaimed. "I have a special guest I'd like to introduce.

"He's a very dear friend of mine, and a most inspirational teacher. Please welcome the one and only Donnie McLeslie!"

Eight hundred people stood on their feet and blasted Donnie with the loudest standing ovation I have ever heard! It went on and on.

"Please sit down everyone," I said. "That's not why Donnie came here today. He's not here to relish his past — that's not his style. This!" I held up a piece of paper. "This is why Donnie came here today." I handed the piece of paper over to Donnie and said, "Read it, Donnie."

Donnie read the poem *If You Think You Can, You Can* by Dr. Denis Waitley.

Instantly, I could see everyone in the crowd getting choked up. As Donnie slowly and methodically read each word I could see more and more people wiping their eyes. Halfway through the poem, Donnie stopped before reading the line "About being an Oakland Raider." There was no way the world's biggest Broncos fan was going to say that out loud. Suddenly, in front of 800 people I had a situation.

"You know the words Oakland Raider?" I asked Donnie

Donnie said, "Yes, I know the words. I no say them."

The crowd was in hysterics, they were laughing and crying at the same time. So, I told Donnie to just change the words.

Although it didn't rhyme, the crowd exploded with cheers after Donnie said, "You can be a Denver Bronco."

Donnie finished the poem by saying, "And I believe I am Unstoppable!"

I stood there with my arm around Donnie the whole time as he read that poem, and I watched 800 people, many of them crying their eyes out!

When he finished, I said, "If Donnie can stand before you today and prove he's not retarded after the 'experts' claimed that he was; if Donnie can read to you and go home and raise two kids; in other words, if Donnie can fill his cup, I challenge you to fill yours!"

At that point, I turned to Donnie and presented him with a framed document that read "Teacher of Inspiration." Donnie got his degree!

Sitting in the middle section of the auditorium, fifteen rows back, was the teacher that called to tell me they had put Donnie in my class...the one who said, "Donnie can't read." We were all there that day to witness Donnie adding another key to his key chain. How many keys are on *your key chain...*

The Unstoppable You believes
if you think you can, or think you can't,
either way, you're right.

Lesson 7

Your Key Chain

"WHAT DO I NEED THIS FOR? I'll never use this stuff after high school!" I can't recall how many times I've heard students say that about some of the classes they take. However, I remember my response, because it was always the same. "Are you a psychic or a fortune teller?" I'd ask. "What crystal ball are you looking into that enables you to foresee and predict your future ten to twenty years from now?"

Far too many high schoolers believe that when they graduate from high school, opportunity will come knocking. They think all they have to do is open the door, walk through, and live happily ever after. Well, my friend, if you believe opportunity will knock, you are believing a myth. Opportunity doesn't come a knockin'. The cold hard reality is that the door of opportunity is locked. The only ones who can open that door are those who have the key.

Education is the key that unlocks the door to opportunity. Every class you take, each new skill you develop or ability you possess, adds yet another key to your key chain.

Everyone's goal should be to get as many keys on your key chain as possible. Because one thing is certain in life: you will come up against locked doors. If you have the right key, you can open the door to opportunity. If you don't have the right key, you're locked out.

In this ever-changing world, it is imperative that you continue this gathering of keys your entire life. That's the only way you'll ever get the most important one, ***the master key...***

The more keys on your key chain, the better the chance of unlocking the door to *The Unstoppable You.*

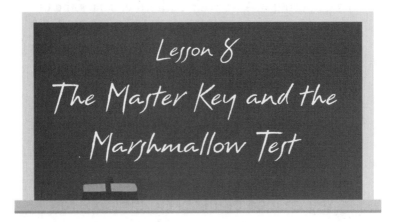

Lesson 8
The Master Key and the Marshmallow Test

EVERY KID GOT ONE as they entered my classroom that Friday. Some of them ate it instantly, a few asked for permission before eating it, while others wondered what a marshmallow had to do with the Friday story, and why I was wearing a huge wooden master key around my neck.

"This master key I'm wearing is the most important key on your key chain," I explained. "The marshmallow is a test to see if you can get your own master key. Today's Friday Story isn't about someone else, it's about you," I said while unveiling a huge marshmallow drawn on the chalkboard with the words, The Marshmallow Test.

Holding Daniel Goleman's book, *Emotional Intelligence*, in my right hand, I proceeded to explain what the marshmallow test was all about.

In 1960 at Stanford University, they performed a now famous experiment. The guinea pigs were a bunch of four-year-old preschoolers. The experiment was to test what Mr. Goleman calls the Master Aptitude, which I call...the Master Key. I wanted to see if my students could figure out what it was they were trying to test.

One by one, they put each youngster in a room. They gave each plucky preschooler one marshmallow. They were told they could eat it right away, but they could only have one. However, if the kids could wait, for what must have seemed like an eternity, for the experimenter to return from his "errand," they could have two! What a temptation — one sure to test the self discipline (master key) of any four year old.

Watching these children resist that temptation must have been hilarious! Some of these kids talked to themselves, covered their eyes, sang, walked around the room, played games with their hands and feet, and even tried to sleep. This group of "master key-ers" demonstrated the self-discipline to receive a second marsh-mallow. Not to be outdone in the comic category was the second group, which grabbed the one marshmallow within seconds of the experimenter leaving the room.

Now for the amazing part! They tracked these two groups all the way till they graduated from high school. As you might have expected, the group that had the master key as preschoolers continued to have self-discipline throughout adolescence. They were not only far superior students, they also had SAT scores 210 points higher than the group that acted on whim. This experiment proved that self-discipline is the master key that will unlock the door when opportunity knocks.

Knowing the important role self-discipline plays in my students' lives, I wanted to challenge them to discover their master key. The test was as simple and basic as the marshmallow test. The outcome was impossible for me to foresee. I guess I never realized how determined some kids would be. I eventually found out after I challenged them to stop talking the talk, and start **walking the walk...**

The Unstoppable You possesses the master key so you can unlock the door to opportunity.

Lesson 9

Walking the Walk

I NEVER OWNED A CAR until I was twenty-one years old. It was an old, beat up, green Ford pickup truck. Since I had no money left after paying for college, Dad cosigned the loan. As we left the bank that day, Dad told me I'd better not miss a payment. I never did. This isn't my sob story — it's how I was raised. If you want it, earn it. I'm O.K. with that.

What I wasn't O.K. with, when I started teaching, was the number of kids that had cars, many of them brand new! Most of them purchased by Mom and Dad. Several times I heard kids say that they wanted a new car for their sixteenth birthday. Plus, they demanded their folks get it for them. Now, a car is a big "want" at age sixteen...big enough that some kids will do anything to get one, including having the discipline to work for it. For those kids, I have always had the utmost respect. But to buy your kid a car just because they turn sixteen robs them of that child's "want." Many parents fail to realize that by giving their kids a car, they are stealing that child's master key. The self-discipline that leads to If you want it, earn it!

One Friday in September, I told my class this story. I don't remember where I first heard it. A father was on his way to work one day when he spotted his eighth-grade son hitching a ride to school. That night at the dinner table, Dad asked his son if he wanted to be a great athlete.

"Of course I do," his son replied.

"Well then, you should be running to school, not hitchin' a ride," Dad said.

"But Dad, we live nine blocks from the school."

"My goodness, I didn't know it was that far! A kid could die in nine blocks!"

Naturally, this teenager responded, "Well, Dad, I guess you walked when you were a kid, didn't you?"

This father, not unlike most fathers, not only said "Yes," but went on to say, "I walked nine miles every morning and nine miles back, uphill both ways. Some days through nine feet of snow."

All good dads embellish the truth from time to time. It's because the older they get, they truly believe the better they were! So, father and son made a deal that night. If the son could walk to school every day, no matter the conditions, he would get a prize.

One dark, dreary morning it was pouring rain outside. Dad was drinking his morning coffee when his son came downstairs and looked out the window. "It sure is raining out there, Dad."

Dad said, "It sure is."

His son said, "Sure looks cold and dreary out there."

Dad said, "It sure does."

"What do you think, Dad?" his boy asked.

"I think you're going to get wet," said Dad.

His son went on to win the prize. "What did he win? What was the prize?" my students always ask. I honestly tell them I don't know what he won. But, perhaps I do...

Many years later, this boy would become a coach. He was flying to Indiana on a recruiting trip. The pilot who was flying the twin engine plane got lost and the plane crashed in the mountains. It was cold, dark, and pouring rain that night. The pilot was killed on impact, and the boy who walked to school climbed out of the wreckage that night as a man. Through the rain, fog, and in the darkness, he saw a light three miles away. This would become the most important walk of his life! He walked to the light, thanks in part to his dad. You see, the real prize he gave his son was the master key. That key, that night, helped his son unlock the most important door of his life.

When I finish telling that story to my class, I give them a warning. "What I'm about to say next is my opinion. That doesn't mean it's right. That doesn't mean it's wrong. It's just my opinion. Having lived in your town for the past many years, I feel I'm qualified to say this. You're spoiled!" I used the student parking lot as evidence to support my claim. "The majority of students who are of legal driving age have cars, many of which are brand new and were just given to them. They never had to work for them."

This really fired 'em up! So much so, that two of them asked for permission to prove me wrong by counting the cars parked in the student parking lot. When they returned, they were slapping each other high fives and laughing. "You were wrong, Mr. Conrad. There's only 197 cars in the student parking lot."

"Only 197," I said.

"That's right," they said.

"And there's about 600 kids in our school," I said. I told them that half of that population was freshman and sophomores. They aren't old enough to drive. So, out of 300 juniors and seniors, almost 200 drive to school each day — many of them with several others in their car. "I think that proves my point," I told them.

That's when the discuss-a-ment heated up. A discuss-a-ment is usually what takes place when you discuss something with a teenager. You have a discussion, they have an argument. It's a dicuss-a-ment. During our discuss-a-ment, one of the boys who counted the cars argued and defended his driving to school, even though he only lived a few blocks away. I kept discussing the advantages of walking to school. I explained the health, financial, and environmental benefits to leaving the vehicle at home. He kept arguing his "need" to drive his truck to school everyday — the truck his dad gave him.

Finally, after sensing he was losing the argument, he screamed, "Well, if it wasn't for my truck, I'd be walking to school every-day!"

I held my arms up in the air and said, "Thank-you!"

Not realizing what he just said, and still pretty hot, he screamed back, "Thanks for what?"

I calmly thanked him again for agreeing with me. I was laughing the whole time. "You just verified what I've been saying this entire time," I chuckled. After he finally realized what he said, he turned and walked away. I was still laughing.

He didn't sign my Master Key list that day. Fifty-some kids did sign up and accepted my crazy challenge to walk to school. Some of our kids live forty miles from town. Those kids opted to do two laps around the track each day. I promised those who completed the challenge a prize when they finished. I would get them a Master Key award; however, I told them they would find their own "real prize" along the way.

That first year of the challenge, there were twenty-seven days where the temperature was below zero or it was snowing. Twenty-seven days of extreme weather conditions. Twenty-seven times the kids could have said, "This is crazy!" Twenty-seven times it would have been easy to quit. Twenty-seven times they could have packed it in. Many did. However, seven of those kids refused to quit.

As promised, those seven kids received their master key awards. They also received a standing ovation from more than 500 people at awards night! That was the prize they received from me. Just wait till you hear what they gave themselves. It's what I told them they would find along the way that would ultimately be ***the real prize...***

Anyone can talk the talk, and many do.
The Unstoppable You walks the walk.

Lesson 10

The Real Prize

WELL OVER FIFTY STUDENTS SIGNED UP to walk each day. Seven of those students stuck with it, and only one of them was a girl. Her name was Michelle Rodewald. Barely 5 feet tall, she was also the smallest in the group. True height, I've told my students many times, isn't your physical height...it's your mental height.

Michelle went home the day of the challenge and told her parents what she had signed up for. Immediately, her mother said, "No way!" Michelle lived several miles from school, and her mother worried about what could happen walking to school each day — especially at night after swim team practice. Not to mention all the "crazies" out there. So, Michelle was told "no."
Although Michelle was short in stature, she was tall in stubbornness. She told her mom she had signed up, and she wasn't about to cross her name off that list. After continued debate, Michelle's mom had no other choice... So, she decided to walk with her.

Each day, Michelle and her mom walked the several miles to school together. There was no phone ringing. There were no brothers asking for another piece of bacon; no husband asking for more coffee. Just Michelle and her mom. Guess what they did each morning on their way to school? You got it! They talked to each other — no distractions. I truly believe this world would be a better place if more parents would take the time to talk to their kids.

I knew the effect it was having on Michelle. What I didn't realize was the effect it had on her mom, but I found out the next year at parent-teacher conferences. Michelle's mom, Debbie, sat across the table and wept unashamedly. Debbie explained how they had gone from being good friends to becoming best of friends. While fighting back my own tears, she told me how much she was going to miss Michelle when she leaves for college. "Mr. Conrad, thank you so much," Debbie said while wiping her eyes.

I said, "You're thanking the wrong person. Thank Michelle."

Josh Roberts and his friend made two commitments the day of the challenge. The first was to walk every day, the second was to each other — to walk together. They followed the same route day after day. One time, during extreme weather conditions, a neighbor along the route stopped the two boys. She asked what they were doing. Months later, this same neighbor would stop me at the grocery store. She told me she and her husband would watch for the boys each day while having their morning coffee. "We could tell what time it was, because they were within minutes of the same time each day," she said. "You could set your clock by it."

Josh used his Master Key after graduating from high school to unlock the door to a musical career. He started a band called The Invisibles. Josh personally delivered the group's first CD to me. I got a little choked up when I read the words on the jacket of the CD cover: "Thanks, Mr. Conrad, for the Master Key. This CD is dedicated to you."

Jamie Mondeau signed up for the two laps each day during his junior year. Since he lived way out of town, he faithfully did his two laps each day after school. Many times I'd yell to him, "Master Key," as I passed the track. One day he had a dentist appointment just before school ended. He had planned to do his laps after the appointment. As usual, the dentist was running late. Jamie had to leave immediately after the appointment to go to work. His job was putting the pepperonis on the pizza at Pizza Hut. He had to close that night, and it was around 11:00 p.m. when he left work. He drove straight home, took a shower, put on his pj's, and was in bed by 11:30. He turned off the light and closed his eyes. That's when it hit him! He needed to do his two laps around the high school track. If he didn't do them tonight, he would have to cross his name off the list. In less than thirty minutes, it would be "tomorrow" and be too late.

Knowing he'd have to move fast, Jamie jumped out of bed and drove to the high school. Still in his pj's and just before midnight, Jamie walked his two laps. It was pitch black outside and the track was covered in snow. I saw his footprints around the track the next morning.

Less than a year later, Jamie would become known throughout the school as "Jumpin' Jammin' Jamie Mondeau." But only after he came ***out of the closet...***

The real prize in life is the one you give to yourself
– that's *The Unstoppable You!*

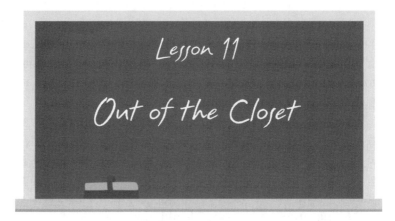

Lesson 11

Out of the Closet

NOT LONG AFTER JAMIE'S MIDNIGHT TREK around the snow-covered track, he had a question for me. "Can I take your woodworking class independent study my senior year?" he asked.

My first response was, "Of course you can, many others have." Normally, kids making huge or complicated woodworking projects sign up for independent study as a way to get another class period each day. I asked Jamie what he was going to make, and was dumbfounded when he told me why he wanted the class. I couldn't believe it! "Are you kidding me?" I mused. In all of my years of teaching, I never even heard of any kids doing that. "Tell me again, why do you want to take this class?"

"I want to play my guitar for an hour each day," Jamie said. He even said it with a straight face.

I knew he had to be joking and said, "Get out of here!"

A few days later he returned. He had the same request. I told him I couldn't help him. I can't play the guitar or read music. My advice was to talk to the band teacher. "Now get out of here," I said for the second time.

I should have realized after Jamie walked the track at midnight — in his pj's through the snow — just how disciplined and determined he was. I mean, in a way, I helped create this monster, because he returned a third time with the same request. Before I had a chance to run him off again, in desperation, he quickly asked, "Mr. Conrad, isn't it true you always say the most important project we work on isn't even made of wood...it's us?"

"Yes, Jamie, that's true," I replied.

"Well then, I want to take your class independent study. I want to improve my guitar playing. I want my 'project' to turn out as good as you do. Besides, the band teacher said no. You're my only chance, Mr. Conrad. Please!"

Finally, I caved in — I think in part because of my secret wish to be a rock and roll star. I made Jamie promise me that if he should ever make it to the "big time," performing at some huge concert, I get the chance to join him on stage. Even though I couldn't play an instrument or sing, I explained I wanted to be there. "I'll play the tambourine," I told him.

"Deal," he said. Then he quickly ran out of my class before I had a chance to change my mind.

That next year, the first day of class, there he was with his guitar. While the rest of the class worked on their projects, Jamie played his guitar. He quickly started sounding good, really good! Some days he would play a song for class. Then one Friday, I decided to surprise and astound all of my classes with a truly unforgettable and "live" Friday Story.

I began by reading to each class Paul Harvey's story, "The Mouse that Roared." This wonderful story was about a second grade teacher, Mrs. Beneduci, and her student, Steven. Mrs. Beneduci was determined to help Steven discover the gift that God had given him. So, with the aid of an unwitting mouse she had placed in the trash can, she asked Steven to help her find it. Steven asked the rest of the class to be super quiet. He then tilted his head from right to left. Steven was drawn to the sound like a bee to honey.

"He's right in here," Steven said pointing to the trash can.

"Well, well, well," said Mrs. Beneduci. "He sure is. Little Steven, you sure are a wonder," exclaimed Mrs. Beneduci.

From that day on, that little blind kid would forever be known as Little Stevie Wonder!

"Mrs. Beneduci helped Little Stevie Wonder discover his gift," I told each class. "Now I'd like to tell you a story about another kid who discovered his gift right here in this very classroom," I told them. I then explained how Jamie took my class independent study, how he played his guitar every day for an hour. I explained in vivid detail how each day Jamie got better and better playing that guitar.

Not only did he play the guitar, Jamie was building one from scratch in his advanced woodworking class. I even held up the instruction book for guitar building. It was over 300 pages thick! "If you follow your passion, it will take you places you have never dreamed of," I said. "And, if you listen very quietly, you can still hear him playing his song." I held my hand up next to my ear as if I were listening. Many of the kids started laughing at my gesture.

Suddenly, from out of nowhere, came the amplified electric sound of Van Halen. Kids looked frantically around the room for the source of the music, but they couldn't find it. I calmly walked over to the closet door, the same closet door where Jamie was patiently waiting for his cue. With his amplifiers hidden from view from his classmates, Jamie jammed away like nothing they had ever heard before.

As I slowly opened up the closet door, I said, "Ladies and gentlemen, let me introduce to you...jumpin', jammin', Jamie Mondeau." From out of the dark closet and into the limelight stepped Jamie.

He literally became a living legend at school his senior year, playing his guitar at all the major sporting events. My personal favorite was his rendition of "The Star Spangled Banner" at the Battle of the Bands. He played it Jimi Hendrix style, with his guitar pick in his teeth. The crowd went ape afterward. I was sitting there thinking, "How cool is that?" I was very proud to say he was in my independent study class.

Jamie continued to work hard playing his guitar the rest of the year. He also worked very hard to complete the guitar he was building. It was one of the most challenging projects ever made in my class. The sweetest, most mellow notes came from that guitar, especially when Jamie played it.

One day early in the summer, when I had come home from work, my wife told me there was something waiting for me in the dining room. When I saw what it was, I became weak in the knees and my eyes started to well up. I couldn't believe it! There on a stand sat Jamie's guitar — the one he made — along with a two page thank-you letter. Immediately after reading the letter, I called Jamie. I told him how much I appreciated his letter but demanded he take back his guitar.

"No way, Mr. Conrad," chuckled Jamie. "What I gave you is nothing compared to what you gave me. Thanks again!"

Jamie's guitar sits in my office. Although it wasn't that expensive to make, its value to me is *priceless...*

The Unstoppable You realizes we all have a gift.
The time has come for you to open yours.

Lesson 12

Priceless

HOMECOMING. Just the thought of it brings fond memories, even for kids still in high school. From the parade, bonfire, the floats, and all the homecoming royalty to the big football game, the dance, and all the festivities...it's the highlight of the school year.

In the Fall of 2004, it looked like homecoming was about to become a disaster, especially for our football team. A few days before the big game, two of our starters got into a fight — with each other! School policy meant they would have to miss the game.

During our pep assembly, another player made an obscene gesture in front of the entire school! He was benched from starting that night. It was beginning to look like our cheerleaders would end up playing the football game. We were running out of players.

That Friday I wanted all of my students, especially the football players, to understand how precious their time in high school is. I asked my class if they've ever had anything stolen from them. Everyone raised their hand.

"How did that make you feel?" was my next question. I can't print what some of them said. Suffice it to say, they were more than upset. "You know what's worse than having something stolen from you?" I asked. "It's when you steal from yourself."

To illustrate this point, I had a huge math equation written on the chalkboard. The equation looked complicated, but the answer was simple. Two hours. That's how much actual playing time occurs during the entire football season. I'm talking *actual* playing time, not standing around in the huddle.

There was a timeline that stretched the entire length of the chalkboard. That timeline represented the 3,000 hours of practice (two a day), bus trips, ecetera, that comprise the football season.

Below that timeline was a much shorter line about a half inch in length. That line represented the two hours of real playing time. How foolish to throw away one second of those precious two hours.

At that point, I asked Scott Garoutte, "What are those two hours worth?" Scott was our stud running back and defensive linebacker. He was also a back-to-back state champion wrestler, as well as an all-state football player. I caught him off guard and put him under some pressure in front of the class.

"Ah...ahh, it's valuable?" Scott stammered. The class erupted with laughter.

"No, it's more than valuable!" I yelled.

"Ah...ahh, it's *really* valuable." Scott was searching for the correct answer. His classmates didn't help any. They were in hysterics.

I asked Scott what he had stolen from him. "Thirty CDs and a CD player," he said. When I asked what he did about it, he told us he bought another one and more CDs.

"Exactly," I said. "Now, what are those two hours worth?"

"Why, they're priceless," Scott said. I explained to him and the entire class that you can't buy those two hours back at any price. Only the foolish would throw away one second by doing something stupid.

What happened next can only be described as divine intervention. Words were coming out of my mouth, but SOMEONE ELSE was doing the talking. If I had not been there myself, I wouldn't have believed it. Wait — I *still* can't believe it!

In front of Scott and twenty-three of his classmates, I said what a pity it would have been if Scott would have done something foolish prohibiting him from playing in tonight's game. "Because I envision you intercepting a pass with less than a minute to go. You will run it all the way in for the game-winning touchdown," I said. "We will beat Rifle for the first time in ten years. You think you would remember that for the rest of your life, Scott?" I added.

"Absolutely," he said.

"What about all those fans? You think they would remember that?"

Once again Scott said, "Absolutely."

That night, the score was tied 7-7 for most of the game. We scored the go-ahead touchdown with two minutes left in the game. We kicked off to Rifle. They marched unimpeded right down the field. With fifty-nine seconds left, they were on our two-yard line. Everyone knew that they would go for two after they scored. They weren't playing to tie: they were going for the win.

Their quarterback dropped back to pass. He threw the ball five yards deep in the end zone. Scott intercepted the football. His first thought was to simply take a knee in the end zone: we would get the ball on the twenty-yard line, and the team could run out the clock. Instead, he told everyone after the game he thought, "Priceless." Scott ran the ball 105 yards for the touchdown — a school record, and one yard short of a state record!

I saw the interception, but I couldn't tell who it was. When I saw that it was number 25, Scott's number, I freaked out! We won the game 21-7! I wasn't the only one freaking out afterward — all of Scott's classmates were running around saying Conrad is going to be off the charts on Monday!

The newspaper did a big article called, "A Priceless Prediction." The whole town knew about the Friday Story. I knew I had to do something special for Scott and his classmates on Monday, and I had a plan. It would be the perfect ending to the lesson of the Friday Story.

Monday, I turned out all the lights in the classroom, having only candles for illumination. I was dressed as a fortune teller. I had a towel wrapped around my head with a big gold star on it and three-inch Christmas ornaments — a moon and a star — as earrings. I was waving my hands over a crystal ball as the kids walked in.

"I knew it, I just knew it," many of them said. Others were laughing too hard. One of them made a wise comment, and I told him to be quiet or I would turn him into a frog.

"The great and magnificent Swami has a question for you, Mr. Garoutte. I know it's impossible, but if it were possible, what would you sell me that touchdown for? I want to be the one running the ball in for the game-winning touchdown. So, how much would you sell it for?" I asked Scott.

Scott sat there, shaking his head. The only thing he said was, "That touchdown was priceless!" Scott's response was the perfect answer to the lesson of the Friday Story. He also realized that physical strength alone is not enough. Mentally, you have to be as **tough as a brick...**

The Unstoppable You treats every day
as if it were priceless, because it is.

Lesson 13

Tough as a Brick

TO THIS DAY, IT IS PROUDLY DISPLAYED in our high school trophy case. Many times I've heard students and others say, "What the heck is a cinderblock doing in the trophy case?" I know why it's there, because I'm the one who put it there. What the students don't know is that cinderblock is a monument from the greatest race ever run at our high school. Certainly, it's the most *famous* race! I've shown the video clip to thousands of people. It's called The Cinderblock Relay. Here's how it happened...

Chris Seick was my student and advisee for four years. I never saw a B on his progress reports or his report card. He was a straight A student, and a great kid — but not the most athletic kid. That's what made The Cinderblock Relay so special. I nicknamed him "Psycho."

One day after school, Chris came to talk to me in the weight room. I think it was the first time he was ever in the weight room, and must have impressed him, because he wanted to return...if I would help him lift. How many times I've been asked that in twenty-six years, I can't remember. I'd help a kid for days, and they would quit after a week or two.

So, I wanted to see how serious Psycho was. "I'm putting you on the thirty-day rule," I told Chris. "You show up here for thirty days in a row, without missing a day, then I'll help you lift." I didn't think he would do it. I was wrong!

After Chris met my challenge, I needed to keep my end of the deal. So, I put him on my workout program. He quickly started getting stronger — much stronger! But physical strength alone is worthless without the mental strength behind it. So, everyday after an hour and a half of working on physical strength, we spent time working on mental strength.

Chris dubbed this time as "The Tricka." The Tricka was basically anything I could conjure up in my mind. I would take all of the weightlifters, some days fifteen to twenty of them, off to do something crazy.

One day it was *The Dumpster Derby*. We pushed a loaded dumpster uphill; the fastest time was the winner. Another day, it was *The Tough Man Contest*. It consisted of all the kids laying in the snow with just shorts on, throwing snow on each other. Did I mention it was 35 degrees below zero that day? It was cool, to say the least.

But the most famous Tricka of all was *The Cinderblock Relay*. This insane event was just like the 400-meter relay, where four runners would each run 100 meters, handing off a baton to each other — but in this case it was a cinderblock. The Cinderblock Relay was my idea. What occurred during the race came from above — literally!

With a windchill of 10 degrees, the runners took their places around the track. As the sky grew dark, I said, "On your mark, get set," and suddenly, hail ripped through the sky. "Go!" Blasting off into an intense pelting and stinging hailstorm, the runners attempted to outrun it. The storm won!

By the time the last runner received the cinderblock, he was barely visible through the hail! The track instantly turned to a carpet of white. How those guys could see, let alone set the new school record, was beyond me.

At the finish line, they unfurled the American flag. The four of them — Chris Seick, Garret Schopper, Al Horrocks, and Brian Skowronski — took their victory lap. Luckily, a fellow teacher decided to film the event. It was a hail of a race! I thought to myself the whole time, "That's just *crazy man...*"

When life rains down on your parade,
The Unstoppable You races on,
finishing in record time.

Author's note: Chris Seick applied his mental toughness to graduate from Colorado School of Mines with a degree in engineering. He is now a metallurgical and materials engineer for an engineering and geology firm. Good job Psycho.

Lesson 14

Crazy Man

THE PROBLEM WITH SOME PEOPLE isn't that they're burned out. Their problem is they were never lit to begin with. I believe the person in charge of our pep assemblies had that problem: the assemblies were lame, and the kids just sat there.

One pep assembly, I appointed myself as faculty cheerleader. Dressed in funky clothing, I came running into the gym with the spirit stick. My goal was to have the kids yell and have fun — that's why they call it a pep assembly! I was acting like a crazy man until someone gave me a megaphone, then I was totally off the charts! Everyone said they never heard it so loud. I achieved my goal.

Most of the student body had a blast; others were very disappointed in me. In fact, when we got back to the classroom, they told me so. "Mr. Conrad, you made a fool out of yourself," one of them said.

"You're right," I fired back. "Please don't take this the wrong way, but I don't care about what you think. Furthermore, the day I quit caring about what you thought of me, is the day I became a better teacher."

An explosion of laughter erupted when one of them asked what I was on. I laughed, too, and told the student I was high on endorphin.

"Can I get some?" he asked.

"Sure," I said. "I can't sell it to you, but I can get you high on endorphin." I didn't explain to the class, at that point, that endorphin is a chemical released by your brain. It's a natural high. I preferred to show them instead.

I told them how every New Year's Eve I would take my wife to Sleepy Cat Guest Ranch for dinner and dancing. At nine o'clock, we would have the dance floor all to ourselves. Even though the place is packed, no one's dancing at nine o'clock — but just before midnight, the dance floor is so crowded you can barely move.

"Why do you suppose that is?" I asked. The students quickly concluded it was the alcohol: many people are too inhibited until they've had a few drinks. They use the alcohol to help them break the chains of inhibition. I went on to explain that since I quit drinking years ago, I no longer needed alcohol to "fuel" my good times. I get fueled by endorphin.

"Since you asked for some, I'll show you how to get it!" I exclaimed. I told the class how every year at Sleepy Cat the song "YMCA" by The Village People would be played. I would lead the crowd, dancing to "YMCA." All of the kids raised their eyebrows and just rolled their eyes.

"Guess what we're going to do today, fellas?" I asked. The room turned to stone silence. "We're going to dance to the song, **'YMCA'...**"

Some people aren't burned out...they were never lit to begin with. *The Unstoppable You* lights up!

I KNEW I WAS IN TROUBLE the second I said it. How in the world was I going to convince a bunch of junior and senior boys to dance to the song "YMCA" — in the wood shop, no less! After all, that song was made famous by the band, The Village People. They weren't the most masculine group in the world!

As I looked around the room, they were all shaking their heads, no way. I had to think fast. I walked straight up to the biggest, strongest kid in the class. His name was Jason, and best of all, he just happened to be wearing a No-Fear T-shirt that day. I asked him to get up and dance with me.

"No way!" was his response. The class roared with laughter.

"Jason, I notice you're wearing a No-Fear shirt. So, you're not afraid of anything?" I asked.

"I ain't afraid of nothing," boasted Jason.

"Well then, stand up and let's dance," I proclaimed.

"No way — that's *gay*," he responded. This brought about an earthquake-rattling round of laughter.

I have to admit, it was pretty funny. I wasn't about to laugh, though. I had a lesson to teach...how to get some endorphin. So, I calmly told Jason to take off his shirt.

"What?" he questioned.

At that point, I went from teacher to actor. I got up in his face; I got super intense. I started screaming, "You say you have no fear! Yet, all I asked you to do is dance. It's not illegal, it's not immoral, yet you don't have the guts to do it! Take off the shirt!" I screamed.

Jason started to get really nervous. "But, Mr. Conrad..." he tried to say.

"But nothing!" I yelled back. "I'll tell you something else. The reason you won't get up is because you're worried about what your classmates will think. And the reason they won't get up is because they're worried about what you're going to think.

"No fear? What a joke! You're an embarrassment to the shirt. Take it off! Take it off!" I screamed at the top of my lungs. I scared the willys out of poor old Jason. He had his shirt halfway off when I turned away, acting all disgusted, and told him to leave it on. "I'm really disappointed with this entire class! Is there not *one* of you that has the guts to stand up and dance? Not *one* of you that has the guts to not worry about what others are going to think?"

Finally, Travis Dove stood up and said, "Ah, what the heck. I'll dance with you, Mr. Conrad." Travis was one of the first kids I taught that had spiky hair and earrings. I think he's the one that started the trend. Once Travis stood up, others around him sheepishly stood up, too. Eventually, every guy in the class — yes, even Jason — was standing.

We did the lamest version of the "YMCA" dance ever. We danced around the table saw and jointer, twenty guys in a dance train, with me in the lead! I often wondered what would have happened had the principal walked in at that exact moment. By the end of the song, we were all laughing, yelling back and forth.

When it was all over, several of them wanted to do it again. I pointed to the class with both hands. "Right there, right now, what you're feeling — that's endorphin! We didn't take any drugs or drink any alcohol, either. This is the *best* kind of high! That's how you get endorphin," I explained. Lesson learned!

Every guy left class that day thinking that that was pretty cool. But the best was yet to come. You see, Travis Dove was about to take that lesson and add ***a touch of class...***

Endorphin is the fuel for *The Unstoppable You!*

Lesson 16

A Touch of Class

A FEW MONTHS AFTER our infamous "YMCA" dance, Travis Dove, the first to stand that day, came to ask me a question. He wanted to know how much I would pay to have my yard mowed. I explained to Travis that I enjoyed mowing my yard. "Besides, I get to pretend I'm the mower, and the grass is all my students," I joked. When I asked Travis, "What's up?" He told me he wanted to start his own lawn mowing business.

That's when I shared an idea with Travis that I'd kept a secret since high school. First, I quizzed Travis to see if he remembered the "YMCA" dance. "How could I ever forget," was his response.

"Do you remember who stood up first that day?" I continued.

"I did," he recalled.

"That's right, Travis. You were the first, and that's why I think you would have the guts to try a gimmick."

Then I asked him what he was going to do to set his business apart from the rest. He said he was going to run an ad in the newspaper. "So will everyone else," I said.

"I'm going to do a great job mowing, and I'll sweep the sidewalks," was his next comment.

"So will everyone else," I said again.

Eventually, Travis exhausted all his ideas and said, "I don't know."

"Well, I do!" I exclaimed.

That's when I told Travis my secret idea. "It's called formal lawn care. You dress in a full tuxedo, top hat and all. You put a sign in each yard while you're mowing that reads Formal Lawn Care. With a touch of class, we cut your grass. What do you think?" I asked.

Travis thought for a second and said, "I like it."

I told Travis that the day he stood up first for the "YMCA" dance was the day that he impressed me. He didn't worry about what other people thought. Most of the other kids in his class would never have had the courage to be different, or to be themselves. They're all looking to fit in, to be a part of the group. In the world of business, different isn't just good — it's essential!

Travis spent weeks gathering up a tux. He went to the thrift store and found pants. He visited yard sales and found a shirt. He bought a jacket at the Bargain Barn. He was so excited the day he found a top hat. "It all matches," he boasted.

Next came the moment of truth. His first yard to mow would be mine, but before that, we had to make a deal. I asked Travis what it would cost him to run an ad in the back of the newspaper.

He said, "About fifty bucks."

Then I asked him what an ad on the front page would cost. He started at one hundred dollars. He stopped guessing when he reached one thousand. The correct answer, I explained to Travis, was no amount of money would get his ad on the front page — that's not what the front page is for.

"I will get your ad on the front page," I told Travis. "All it's going to cost you is your time. I'm going to let you mow my yard for free."

"Say that again," a confused Travis said.

"You heard me," I said. "I'm going to let you use my mower. I'll fill it with gas. In exchange, I'll not only get you on the front page of the newspaper, I'll get you on local TV. Just show up at my house with your tuxedo and sign at 5:00 p.m."

I had to laugh when I saw him in his tux for the first time. I was thinking how outrageous all this was as Travis started the mower. I live on the main street of town, and my yard is eight city lots. It's huge! I knew Travis would get plenty of attention. I just didn't expect there would be cars crashing into each other. Seriously, it almost happened!

Some drivers stopped in the middle of the street. Others honked their horns. Everyone waved as they slowed to a crawl to watch this boy in the tux. A friend of my wife, Vicki, called our house to ask if we knew there was a guy mowing our yard in a tux!

In the midst of this pandemonium, I called the newspaper. I said, "Some dude is mowing a yard on Yampa Avenue in a tux. You gotta check it out! He's stopping traffic!" The newspaper said they would be there right away. My next call was to the local TV station. I gave them the same line I gave the newspaper.

When I finally got back outside, what a sight! The photographer from the newspaper was snapping shots of Travis. The TV crew was chasing him around with the camera. Cars had pulled off to the side of the street. People were standing on the sidewalk pointing at him. The whole time, Travis kept mowing, just like I told him, in his little tuxedo and top hat. His sign in the yard said Formal Lawn Care. "We got the class to cut your grass."

The next day, on the front page of the *Craig Daily Press* was a picture of Travis. The picture was about one-quarter the size of the front page. It was gigantic! The best part was the caption, which read:

> ### *"We've Got the Class to Cut Your Grass"*
> Travis Dove, a senior at MCHS, takes a formal approach to lawn care yesterday afternoon at Craig Conrad's home on Yampa Avenue. Dove and Conrad came up with the idea in one of Conrad's Friday Stories about breaking the chains of inhibition. "I figured he'd have the initiative to try a gimmick," said Conrad. Dove said he charges between $10.00 and $15.00 to cut a lawn, depending on the size. He plans to continue his business through the summer. Mowing lawns in a tuxedo is "kinda hard, but not that bad," said Dove.

That article, along with the television interview, got Travis's phone ringing off the hook. Eventually, Travis called me in a panic. "Mr. Conrad," he said in desperation, "I can't handle all the lawns I'm getting."

"Travis," I said, "hire some kid to help you and pay him $10.00 and charge the customer $15.00. You can make $5.00 and go drink *lemonade...*"

Dare to be different, dare to be yourself.
That's what makes *The Unstoppable You!*

Lesson 17

Lemonade

I CAN STILL RECALL MY "FIRST" TASTE of being an entrepreneur. It happened in second grade on Lincoln Road in Berks County, Pennsylvania. "The Kids," as we were called, decided to earn our own money selling handpicked raspberries and cherries at our roadside stand. Unfortunately, there wasn't much traffic on that backcountry road, and we literally ended up eating most of our profits. What a sight it must have been to the few customers who did stop, seeing all those little kids with purple fingers and purple lips! Some laughed so hard that they paid full price for a half-eaten box of raspberries! That first "taste" stayed with me all of my life. That's the reason why, while riding my bike in the summer of 2004, I decided to stop at the lemonade stand I saw that day.

The first question I asked those two budding entrepreneurs was, "Do you know why I stopped here today?"

"Because you're thirsty?" they said in unison.

"True," I said "but there's another reason. Do you guys know what an entrepreneur is?"

They gave each other a confused look and sheepishly said, "No."

I explained what an entrepreneur was, and how much I admired their spirit. "After all, what are your friends doing today?" I asked.

"They're sleeping or at the pool," John Kirk replied.

I said, "But not you two. You're out here in the hot sun with your little sign trying to earn some money, and I dig that! You see, I've always had my own business, so I can fully appreciate your willingness to improve your financial situation." They gave each other another confused look. "Now, as an entrepreneur myself, I'm always looking for a deal. So what special deal are you going to give me?"

They whispered to each other and said, "We'll throw in a free piece of bubble gum."

"Deal!" I said, as I plunked down my fifty cents. They quickly put it in their little cigar box with the rest of their profits from the day.

As I drank my lemonade I asked, "What are you earning the money for?"

John's sister, Hannah, said she lost a book and owed the library $12. Her parents were making her pay for it.

"Good parents," I told Hannah. "They're teaching you responsibility. What about you, John?"

"I'm saving 'til I get $11."

"What do you need $11 for?"

"I want to buy an old truck inner tube to float the river."

"Hey, I have one I'll sell you for $2," I told him. John's eyes lit up like he had just opened a Christmas gift!

"Are you serious?" he asked excitedly.

"Sure." I said. "Now go ask your mom if you can ride over to my house to get it. And don't forget your $2." He ran!

I figured I had better go introduce myself to Mom, and that's when I found out what John was really going to do with the inner tube.

"He's inventing a float tube to fish from," his mom told me. Now I shared John's excitement, being a fly-fisherman myself — a fact that John's mom shared with her son.

As we rode to my house, we talked about how cool his invention would be, and how we could fish together someday. We parked our bikes against the wood pile next to my shed, and I was praying that I still had that old tube, because at that point, I was willing to buy him a new one if I had thrown mine out.

Much to my relief, after rooting around in the top of my shed, I saw it. "I found it!" I yelled.

"Perfect!" John said, as he tried stuffing it into his backpack — only it was so big that it wouldn't fit! So, he wrapped it around his neck and hurried home...but not before he paid me $3. "You can keep the extra dollar, it was worth it!" John said.

As John rode off, I reflected back to my first taste of entrepreneurship when I was younger. I hoped John's experience was at least as sweet as what I was chewing on — that free piece of **bubble gum...**

The Unstoppable You always practices the win/win in all dealings with others.

Lesson 18

Bubble Gum

I KNEW SOMETHING WAS ABOUT TO HAPPEN the minute they stepped out of the van. Three adult couples, all drinking beer, walked into Taco Johns. While continuing to drink their beer, they placed their order. I quickly reasoned that if the parents were this undisciplined, what were the seven little kids going to be like that followed them in. It didn't take long to find out...

Instantly, they were drawn to the bubble gum machines, like moths to the light. Seven little monsters attacked. They tried turning the handles and lifting the doors in hopes of getting a free prize. None of them had any money. However, that didn't stop 'em. They clamored all over those machines until suddenly...

The oldest one of the group accidentally discovered the lid to the biggest machine of all wasn't locked. He just lifted it off. Low and behold, directly underneath that lid were all the little treasures that seconds before were *locked away*. Now, they were free for the taking. At first, all seven stopped what they were doing, perhaps in disbelief of their new-found gold mine and the opportunity that waited.

I watched foolishly, thinking maybe one of them would have the discipline to tell their parents or the manager. I was wrong. In a scene that could best be described as a shark feeding frenzy, they attacked. Seven vicious sharks, all trying to reach inside with both fins.

Bubble gum and prizes were falling to the floor as they stuffed their pockets to the brim. In true pecking order, the smaller sharks had to circle around the bigger ones, picking up the scraps.

Sitting beside me the entire time was my three-year-old son, Colton. He didn't nudge me and say, "Check it out, pops. Those guys don't have the Master Key (self-discipline)." Are you kidding? He wanted to join in, too! So, I gave him the "look." You parents know what I mean: you don't have to say a word. You just give 'em the evil eye. He sat down.

The feeding frenzy continued, with no let up. In the chaos, one of the plastic toy containers rolled across the floor where Colton was sitting. He looked at me with pitiful eyes. I gave him the look again, while shaking my head, no. What a mean Dad!

The parents, oblivious to the commotion — perhaps because they were drunk — continued drinking and ordering their food. Finally, one of the mothers saw the aftermath and told the kids to "put 'em back." Ah, the moment of truth. What would these little sharks do? Can a feeding frenzy be reversed, I wondered? Slowly and very reluctantly, the sharks gave back their "prey."

As they filled the machine back up with the prizes, I watched one little girl. She stuffed her favorite prize deep into her pocket. When asked if she put it all back, she said nothing. She nodded her head, yes. I watched really closely: did I just see her nose grow? Like **Pinocchio...**

The Unstoppable You knows the apple doesn't fall too far from the tree. How are your apples?

Lesson 19

Pinocchio

PINOCCHIO. It was the first motion picture I ever saw. It was also my favorite. My grandmother took me on the bus to see it that day. We went to the Majestic Theater in Reading, Pennsylvania. Some of those images stayed with me forever — the whale, Jiminy Cricket, Geppetto, and the odyssey that would test the wooden puppet's bravery, loyalty, and honesty. Is it any wonder when it was first released on home video that I immediately ran out and bought it? Most people believed I got it for my preschooler. Nope, I got it for me. I use it once a year on a Friday...

I explain to my classes that Walt Disney was a genius. He understood the significance of the Master Key, or what I call self-discipline. He did a marvelous job of teaching it through cartoons. I then play that clip to my class.

Pinocchio befriends a roguish character named Lampwick. Together they head off to Pleasure Isle, a place with no rules, no discipline. It's like the Spring Break version of "Puppets Gone Wild." Pinocchio is easily lead astray: he drinks, smokes, and plays pool, despite the warnings of his conscience, Jiminy Cricket.

Left to their own accord, with no discipline, all of these bad boys soon make jackasses out of themselves. If not for the split-second heroics of Jiminy Cricket, Pinocchio was destined to become a jackass, too! I believe the message old Walt was trying to explain was simple: without discipline (the Master Key), you, too, will make a jackass out of yourself.

I then ask my class this question, "How many of you failed to listen to your conscience, only to make a jackass out of yourself?" Every single hand goes up. "You are not alone, my young friends, for I, too, have a story to tell. It was supposed to be a story about roasting weenies. Unfortunately, all we got out of it was **toasted buns...**"

Without self-discipline, *The Unstoppable You* will turn into a jackass, too!

Lesson 20

Toasted Buns

HONESTLY, ALL WE REALLY WANTED TO DO THAT DAY was roast some weenies. We never expected to get our buns toasted — in front of the whole wide world, no less! Looking back on it now, I know it was a good thing...those toasted buns.

They say the apple doesn't fall too far from the tree. My dad was like a huge apple tree. I guess it was just his way of growing good apples.

Many times my brother, Kevin, and I asked Dad for matches. But every time, the answer was the same, "No!"

So, we would beg. "Please, we just want to cook some hot dogs outside of our log cabin fort, the one we built up in the woods."

We had Dad's answer memorized. "No way. You kids will burn it down," he told us for the millionth time.

Amazingly, one day while walking home from elementary school Kevin found a pack of matches. God was on our side! We could have our fire. I asked my cousins, Jerry and Bobby, to help us. After all, this was going to be a ceremonial first fire. We were going to "break in" our fireplace.

The four of us devised a plan. We had to do it right: after all, we might never get another chance, we reasoned. How prophetic that would later become. Since all four of us had watched the Olympics on TV that summer, we decided on the torch technique. This was going to be cool!

Grabbing fistfuls of dry grass, we made our torches. Next, we spread out in a line. Each of us was about fifty yards apart. Kevin got to light his torch first, because he found the matches. He ran and passed the flame to Bobby. Bobby ran and passed the flame to Jerry. Jerry passed the flame to me. I ran with pride, having been chosen for the honor of lighting the first fire in our fireplace. I ran fast.

That dash provided my first lesson on fire and oxygen. The faster I ran, the hotter my torch burned. So, I ran faster. Unfortunately, not fast enough! I was running out of torch. Sensing I wasn't going to make it all the way, I threw the flame toward the fireplace. It didn't quite make it. Most of what was left of my fiery torch landed inside the fort. Did I mention that we carpeted the inside with sixteen inches of dry grass for comfort?

At first, I was too concerned about my hot hand to notice we had our fire. Boy, did we *ever*! It was almost as if we had soaked our little fort with kerosene. Instantly, the flames were shooting through the roof. A shroud of panic engulfed the four of us. We were running around in circles, crashing into each other, trying to squelch the flame. It was all in vain. The fire spread. Now the old dead tree, next to the fort, was on fire. More panic.

I ran to my house. I knocked on my own front door. Mom looked confused as she said, "What is it, Craig?" Then she saw the flames. They weren't hard to miss. They were about twenty to thirty feet high and spreading.

"Oh, my God! George, George!" she yelled upstairs to my dad. "The kids set the woods on fire!" I didn't feel like I should correct her at that point. It was actually our *fort* that was on fire... well, *and* that big tree, too. Dad had just gotten home from work. He was taking a bath. He always liked to relax in the tub. Now, he wasn't relaxed.

He roared incoherent words as he splashed his way downstairs. He was drippin' wet with only a towel wrapped around him when he saw the flames for the first time. More roaring, more incoherent words...only louder!

Mom got on the phone. She called my aunt and uncle, Jerry and Bobby's mom and dad. Together, the four of them fought the flames for hours. Using buckets and shovels, they ran back and forth from the house to fill up with water, and then back to the fire. It was a distance of over two hundred yards. My job was to fill the buckets.

The entire time Dad didn't talk, not a word. Only after the fire was out did he speak. When he spoke, he spoke to the crowd. Word of the fire had spread, almost as fast as the fire itself. Now all my relatives were there — my grandparents, my cousins — Kelly and Kari — and my other aunt and uncle.

All were assembled to hear Dad ask, "Anyone want to see a show?" I couldn't believe it. I thought he was going to be upset. Instead, he was talking about going to the movies.

"Yeah, yeah, we want to see a show!" my brother and I yelled along with everyone else. While reeling us in with one finger, he called for my brother and I. Slowly, I started to become aware of the fact that we were not going to the movies. We were about to *become* the show.

He picked me first. As I walked toward him, I could see the black specks of soot stuck on his forehead. I watched the sweat dripping from his nose. Looking up at him, he seemed as tall as the tree we just burned down. From behind me, I could hear the snickers of all of my relatives.

"Yes, Dad," I said.

"Pull down your pants," he said while slowly pulling off his belt. The snickers behind me turned to laughter. The audience was enjoying the show. They were going to get their money's worth, because Dad was about to utter the two words I feared the most — "underwear, too!"

I tried to plead…"But, but, Kelly and Kari are watching." That didn't matter.

"Underwear, too!" he said for the second time. As I reluctantly pulled my underwear down to my ankles, the laughter intensified. I was totally "in-bare-assed"! I could feel the sun's warm rays on my skinny little butt cheeks. I knew those cheeks were about to get a lot warmer. Dad snapped the belt straps together — the sound of leather cracking against leather. The pain that was on my mind would soon be on my behind. Dad asked if I remembered why he wouldn't let us build a fire in our fireplace.

"Because we could burn down the fort," I trembled.

"Well, you're right. You just did." He went on to say, "Now, this hurts me more than it's going to hurt you." That had to be the craziest thing I ever heard as a kid. Dad would say it each time he disciplined us. Why was I the only one crying? Everyone else was in tears laughing.

As Dad readied his swing, I was left with only one option. I would scrunch my butt cheeks tightly together to lessen the pain, a trick I had learned from experience. Dad knew about my trick, so he waited until I couldn't hold it any longer. The sight of my little cheeks flexing, then unflexing, had my relatives in hysterics. Many were rolling on the ground. I was thinking, "come on, get it over with! Just do it!"

The sudden sting of leather reminded me to be careful what you wish for. Even though Dad didn't swing that hard, I let out a blood curdling scream! I tried to run. You ever try to run with your pants down around your ankles? I tripped and fell. Dad managed to get a couple of shots on my behind as I rolled around on the ground along with the rest of my relatives. When it was over, I ran crying to the back of the house.

Soon, the entire scenario was repeated. I could hear the laughter and the screams as my brother took his turn. We met on the back porch. We planned to run away from home. There was just one big obstacle in our plan. The only other home we had, we had just burned to the ground. With our pride hurting more than our rear ends actually did, we decided to stay home. Like I said — all we really wanted to do was roast some weenies. Instead, we got our buns toasted!

Years later, I would thank Dad for disciplining us. After twenty-six years of teaching high school, I've seen how kids end up who have had no discipline when they were younger. Thanks, Dad.

Now you think we would have learned our lesson that day. For the most part, we did. It wasn't until high school that we would fall victim to Dad's favorite saying, ***"The masses are the asses..."***

Without discipline, a kid can never grow up
to be *The Unstoppable You!*

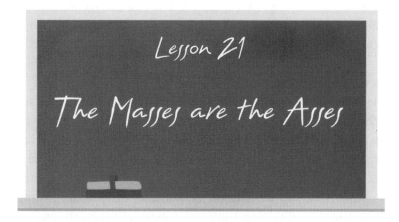

Lesson 21

The Masses are the Asses

THEY WERE THE BULLIES OF THE SCHOOL BUS. Now they were bullying us. "We're going to raid your house tonight," the Schwartz brothers threatened.

Tonight was Halloween night. Raiding houses usually consisted of soaping windows, throwing cattle corn, and spreading toilet paper. But, with the Schwartz boys, Lord only knows what else they'd do... These were the same two guys who were thrown off the school bus one day for jacking around, and had to walk miles to get home. They both cussed at the poor old driver as they were getting the boot. I didn't care for either one of 'em.

We told Dad of the pending attack the Schwartz brothers were planning just as soon as we got off the bus. We also told him that the best defense would be a good offense. We wanted to attack first. Kevin and I showed Dad the sack of corn we had hand peeled and the bars of soap we had gathered. We were ready, totally prepared. All we needed was the car. I was old enough to drive and we'd be careful, I promised Dad.

"Could we borrow the car keys?" I asked. Dad refused. Never once during our entire childhood did my brother and I ever get a chance to go raiding.

"Why don't we ever get to do what all the other kids are doing?" I cried.

"Because the masses are the asses," Dad fired back. It was one of his favorite sayings. He'd repeat it whenever we wanted to do something that all the other kids were doing, especially if he disagreed with it.

Forlorn and rejected, my brother and I devised Plan B. Together, we reasoned and rationalized that if we couldn't raid other people's houses, we would raid our own house. We would teach Dad a lesson, too! It was the perfect plan. We had already laid the groundwork about the Schwartz brothers, so we could blame it all on them. Our sister, Jodi, would have to clean up the mess — an added bonus. Perfect!

After dinner, we discreetly stashed our raiding supplies upstairs in Kevin's bedroom. His room was directly above the living room, and Mom and Dad would be watching TV in there when we attacked.

Just before we went to bed, we put a bug in Dad's ear. "Watch out for the Schwartz brothers. Who knows what they'll do tonight. Goodnight," we said as we trudged upstairs. We slammed our doors loud enough so George and Delores could hear we were in our separate bedrooms.

After fifteen minutes or so, I could faintly hear the sound of the TV come on in the living room. Mom and Dad were taking their places for the night. It was time for us to take our places, too!

The hinges creaked as I slowly opened the door and tiptoed over to Kevin's room. "Did they hear you?" Kevin asked.

"No way, the TV's too loud." I was trying not to laugh.

This was already fun, and about to become hilarious. Together, we shimmied open Kevin's bedroom windows. Trying hard not to laugh out loud, we reached into the sack of shelled corn with both hands. Some of the kernels slipped through our fingers to the floor as we leaned out the window. For sure, we would need to pick up that evidence before morning.

"On the count of three," I whispered to Kevin.

We were both on the verge of busting up with laughter. One, two, three...we pelted the windows with corn. Although it does no damage to the windows, it scares the heck out of anyone sitting nearby.

We heard Mom gasp. George got up. We knew exactly what he'd do. He had a routine we'd seen a hundred times before. First, he turns on the floodlights outside. On came the lights as I tiptoed back to bed. Next, the dogs would start barking. Barking dogs right on cue, I thought as I pulled the covers up over my head. Then Dad would run to the gun cabinet, load his shotgun, and go outside.

We lived on a small farm in a rural part of Pennsylvania. The nearest house was over a quarter of a mile away. To call the police would be a waste of time. I never saw a cop drive by the farm in all the years I lived there. Besides, we didn't need cops — we had George. He thought he was the law — at least the law of Limekiln, the little hamlet in which we lived.

Dad's law was shoot first, ask questions later — especially when it came to his property that he worked so hard to attain. I remember some nights when the dogs started barking, Dad would fire a few warning shots into the air. It was his way of letting would-be intruders know he was the law 'round these parts. I don't know if it actually scared anyone, but it sure made Dad feel good. Perhaps it was all those John Wayne movies. Afterward, he'd strut into the house and declare the property free of all perpetrators.

I heard the door close. Dad was back in the house. Immediately, he raced up the stairs to my bedroom. "Craig, Craig — the Schwartz boys hit the house," he panted.

Faking like I was asleep and trying not to smile, I rolled over in a slumber and said, "I told you."

When Dad got back downstairs, I could hear my brother laughing so hard I was scared my folks could hear him.

"Shut up," I whispered across the hall.

This was just the beginning. Next was round two. After Dad settled down, I snuck back over to my brother's room. We couldn't even look at each other for fear of cracking up. Simultaneously, we reached into the sack again. With even more corn spilling to the floor, we fired a second round — we fired a third and a fourth round, too! What the heck, we were having too much fun to stop now!

Again Mom screamed. Dad got up and turned on the lights. I could tell he was running. So was I, on my tiptoes. I dove under my covers. The dogs were going crazy. Then suddenly — boom, boom — Dad fired two shots! I almost wet the bed. My brother was laughing so loud I thought Dad would hear him for sure, and he was outside the house.

I was in pain trying to hold it all in. I was having trouble breathing, trying to catch my breath. When Dad got back in the house, I could hear him running up the stairs to my room. I panicked. "What do I do now?" I thought as Dad turned on my light. I buried my face so deep into my pillow that I couldn't breathe.

Dad shook me violently to wake me. "Craig, Craig — the Schwartz boys are hiding outside! They hit us again!" the lawman said in a panic.

I couldn't even turn around. If I did, Dad would have seen the tears streaming down my face. I stayed buried. Only after he left to go into Kevin's room could I get some air. I remember praying that Kevin wouldn't blow our cover. He didn't. Dad gave up and surrendered back to the living room.

Later, my brother and I rendezvoused in the upstairs bathroom. It was time for the coup de grace! We opened up the bathroom window and crawled out unto the porch roof. We climbed down the tree that grew next to the porch, like a couple of chimpanzees. We were outside, ready to do some monkeying around. Finally, we could laugh out loud — and we did. The thought of us outside the house and Mom and Dad inside the house just added to the hysterics.

We nodded to each other as we removed the bars of soap from our pockets. The pride we felt in having successfully raided our own house would soon be complete. Knowing it was Jodi's job to clean the windows, we humored ourselves with that image of our sister cleaning all the ones we were soaping. We even soaped the car windows.

I started climbing the tree to get back into the house when Kevin decided to soap the living room windows.

"No, don't be an idiot. Mom and Dad are sitting right there!" I said. My brother never listened to me before, and he didn't listen to me now, either.

"I'll be quiet," he said reassuringly as he walked over to soap the living room windows.

I was just about on the porch roof when I saw my brother come flying around the house.

"Run, Run! I banged the soap against the window!" he yelled.

"You *?!* idiot!" I said as I made my way to the bathroom window.

I was halfway in the window when the front door burst open.

There he was, the "Law of Limekiln" with his twelve-gauge shotgun. In the dimly lit moonlight, Dad observes one "Schwartz brother" climbing the tree and the other "Schwartz brother" climbing through the window into his house. Now's not the time for questions, it's a time for shooting.

"Freeze, or I'll shoot!" Dad yelled as he shouldered his shotgun.

I bumped my head hard on the bathroom window as I tried to raise my arms like someone under arrest.

"Don't shoot Dad, it's us!" I pleaded.

"Craig, Kevin — is that *you*?" Dad said while shaking his head as if to remove the cobwebs.

"Yes, don't shoot!" I said, standing up slowly with my arms raised high above my head.

It wasn't until the next day that we all got a good laugh out of the whole thing. However, my sister Jodi got the best laugh of all. She slept through the whole ordeal, and she laughed the entire time while she sat there on the porch, watching Kevin and I clean windows.

Even though my dad's name is George, that wouldn't be the last time a guy named George would point a loaded gun at me. The next time it would be **Psycho George...**

The Unstoppable You passes the masses,
climbing up the ladder of success.

Lesson 22

Psycho George

1985 WAS QUITE A YEAR! In addition to getting RIFed from my teaching job, we bought our first house that summer, and it wasn't your typical starter home. It sat on eight city lots. Built in 1889, it was an old Victorian that needed tons of work. The property also had a duplex apartment and five other rental cottages. All of those units were dilapidated as well.

I was confident I could take on this humungous renovation project because of the skills I was gaining as a maintenance man for our school district. I was a little less confident about George. His last name was Swatko. He was seventy-two years old and had been living in one of those run-down cottages for the past twelve years. I had never met George until after we closed on the house. The previous owners tried to downplay his looks as we left the abstract office.

I met George for the first time a couple of weeks after we moved in. He gave me the creeps. He looked very disheveled with his shirt unbuttoned and shoes untied. His face was whiskered from days without a razor, his old gray hair was long, oily, and very stringy. As we approached each other, it became obvious he didn't bathe often. He reeked so badly, you could smell him outside when he had his apartment door open! That's not an exaggeration. He also rode a motorcycle.

It was rumored that years before he moved in, someone was murdered in his apartment. Although I never believed much in ghosts, the apartment did appear to be haunted, judging by George's looks! Some of my students called him Freddy Krueger, named after the gruesome, ghoulish character from the movie, *A Nightmare on Elm Street.* We inherited George on the day we bought the house.

In the beginning, everything was cool. Even though he was scary to look at, George was friendly to talk to. He never asked me to fix anything inside his apartment. Since I didn't even have a key, I never *saw* the inside for five years! I was shocked and appalled when he invited me in for the first time! The stench was overwhelming! The walls were brown from cigarette smoke. The carpet was worn down to the backing, the floor covered with dirt. The gas line to the heater and hot water tank leaked. His solution was to light a match at the leak to burn it off. This created a burning flame at each leak, an unbelievable fire and safety hazard! I offered to fix the place up, but George wouldn't hear of it.

Each month he paid his rent early, and never once did he cause a problem. I even made a comment one day that George was our best tenant.

"Why couldn't they all be like George?" I said to my wife, Vicki.

Two years later, I would realize I was wrong, almost "dead wrong"!

Spring

We invited George to come inside our home many times. He never did. Then one spring day in May 1990, he asked to come in. He was crying and visibly shaken. "I talked to Vera today at the Kum and Go," he began. Vera and her husband, Fred, owned our property back when George first moved in many years ago. "She pointed at my shoes and said I looked like a homeless person," he sobbed as tears rolled down his cheeks. George's shoes were so old and worn that they were more like sandals. His toes were sticking out. "What did she mean by that?" he questioned me.

I was caught off guard. I thought maybe he was pulling my leg.

"I don't know, George. I'm sure she was just joking with you," I said.

George raised his voice, "No, she wasn't!"

He became even more upset. I tried to console him by asking what *he* thought she meant when she called him homeless.

"You're either kicking me out, or they're burning the place down!" he cried.

I couldn't believe what I was hearing. George believed Fred and Vera still owned the property. He remembered that some other property they had owned "mysteriously" caught fire years ago. Vera's "homeless" comment caused George to think he was next. For the next hour, I tried to convince George that he was not going to be homeless.

"You've seen me mowing the yard and fixing up the place for the last five years, haven't you George?" I asked. "Fred and Vera don't own this property anymore, I do. No one's going to burn it down, and I'm not kicking you out," I told him.

Eventually he stopped crying, and I patted him on the back as he left.

"Everything is going to be okay, George," I said.

As I closed the door, I thought, "That was weird!" But, things were about to get weirder...

Summer

That summer, George got a telephone for the first time since he lived in the apartment. He used it as a weapon. He would call the local bar and grill, where he had started to drink again. He would rage at the waitresses over the phone and tell them to quit calling him late at night. This alarmed the waitresses, because they had never called George. They didn't even know who he was.

Later that summer, he was sure his phone had been tapped and someone was listening to his conversations. He would call my wife Vicki at home during the day and have bizarre conversations about being in her French class. He wasn't even in her French class.

One day when Vicki went over to give him the newspaper to read, George came to the door wearing only his underwear. He was carrying a pistol, too! He kept asking her, "Where's Craig? Where's Craig?" That was the final straw that freaked us both out.

I truly believed George was losing his mind, which was verified when I heard him having loud conversations with himself as I walked by his apartment.

"Don't ever go over there again," I told my wife.

Fall

On Monday, September 24, I was home splitting firewood after school. The previous day Rich Sadvar, one of my former students, and I were cutting firewood in the mountains when we heard calls for help. Running to the scene, we encountered a man who had cut down a tree, which had fallen on him. His leg was badly broken in three places, and the bone was sticking out of his cowboy boot. After splinting his leg and carrying him to his truck, his wife drove him to the hospital. On our way home, Rich and I got into a conversation about how gross that poor guy's leg was.

Rich asked me, "You gonna have nightmares?"

"Nope, the only thing that gives me nightmares are psychos — people that lose their mind and would kill you without thinking twice," I said.

Ironically, I was about to come face-to-face with my worst nightmare, in the middle of the day...

I could see George out of the corner of my eye coming toward me as I was splitting firewood. I could tell he was drunk. He started cussing about being homeless again.

Ranting and raving, he swore, "When I go, I'm taking somebody with me!"

"Here we go again," I thought as George stormed back to his apartment.

Meanwhile, Vicki came outside to talk to me. She was carrying our ten-month-old son, Colton. Thank God he started to cry: he needed his diaper changed. As Vicki was headed back inside the house, she passed George — who was coming back for round two.

"I was talking pretty tough awhile ago," he slurred with the help of the alcohol he had been drinking. "I always believed if you're going to talk tough, you gotta back it up. And I can back it up," he said while pulling his pistol from beneath his shirt. He started waving it in my direction.

At first, he wanted to go "get Vera." When I asked him why, he mumbled something about fire and homeless. I knew for a fact that George was drunk, and I sensed he was crazy. Any minute, Vicki would be coming outside with Colton. I was terrified what George might do.

Standing there with only a log in my hands, I calmly said to George, "Put away your gun now."

Instead of calming him, he became enraged.

"You gonna make me," he threatened.

"No, I'm not going to..." I tried to say.

George raised his pistol. He pointed it right at my head. I could see the bullets in the cylinder.

"Let's go, let's get it on!" he said.

I will never forget the sound of the metallic click as he pulled back the hammer. His hand was trembling, my heart was pounding. What happened next can only be described as ***an act of God...***

That which doesn't kill you, only makes
The Unstoppable You stronger!

Lesson 23

An Act of God

THERE'S NOT A WHOLE LOT OF TIME TO THINK when someone has a loaded gun pointed at your head — specially once they
pull back the hammer. Now's not the time for talking — it's time
to react. It all comes down to the most basic of animal instincts...
fight or flight. Had Vicki and Colton been there, the only choice
would have been to fight. Luckily, she was still inside changing his
diaper. So, I chose the other option — flight.

I ran away while zigzagging, so I'd be harder to hit. My shoulder blades nearly touched with tension in anticipation of being
shot. As I was running, I had a weird thought. "I'll feel the bullet
before I hear the gunshot." I zigzagged until I got clear across 8th
Street. "He'd have to be a good shot to hit me from here," I thought
as I turned around to see where George was. He was headed back
inside his apartment. To this day, I don't know if the gun jammed
or if he decided not to shoot.

I ran in the front door of my house. Vicki had Colton on the
floor in the middle of changing his diaper.

I yelled to her, "George just tried to shoot me," as I ran upstairs
to load my double barrel shotgun. "What should I do?"

"Call the police," Vicki calmly replied.

Only after I loaded my gun did I call 911. I had the phone
in one hand and a loaded twelve-gauge shotgun in the other. The
police were on their way when the phone rang. It was George.

"Let's call a truce," he said.

My scared and sarcastic response was truce, peace, love, whatever. "What the heck did I do that caused you to try to shoot me?" I yelled into the phone.

"You've been bugging my phone and reading my mail by sneaking into my apartment," he claimed.

"I don't even have a key to your place!" I screamed back.

My heart was pounding and my mind was racing! Suddenly, I got very calm.

"I have an idea, George." Suppose I call the cops and have them check the lock and dust for fingerprints. We'll see if we can catch whoever it is that's getting into your apartment."

"Good idea," he said as he slammed the phone down.

The police would later give credit to that quick thinking for preventing a shootout with George. When they arrived, he thought they were coming to dust for fingerprints. Instead, they arrested him. His loaded gun lay on the table next to the door.

As the police handcuffed and escorted George to the police station, a terrifying realization set in. What's next? Obviously George would figure out I tricked him when I called the police. This would totally convince him that I was the boogeyman. I knew what the police would do. George was seventy-two years old. A slap on the wrist, maybe a night in jail, then "Psycho George" would be coming home.

We had to go to the police station to make a statement. I told Vicki that once we got home, to go ahead and take Colton and leave for a week, month, or a year. I was sure that the problem with George would escalate to a shootout. I didn't want them to be innocent victims. On the way to the police station, I prayed harder than I ever had. I needed help...

We could see George through the mirrored glass as we entered the police station. He couldn't see us. They were beginning their interrogation. We were led to the statement room.

Suddenly, the officers who were with George started screaming for the officer who was with us. Our officer ran to the room that George was in. Police cars were pulling up to the police station with their lights and sirens on. Next came the ambulance.

Police and paramedics were frantically scrambling and yelling in a state of confusion. I thought George freaked out, grabbed an officer's gun and shot someone.

My wife was hiding in the bathroom with Colton in her arms, and I was guarding the doorway. He would have to kill me first. For almost half an hour, I stood guard not knowing what was going on. When the door slowly opened, an officer was standing there, white as a ghost.

"Did this guy ever have any health problems?" he asked.

"What the heck is going on?" I exclaimed.

"George dropped over," he told us. The ambulance just rushed him to the hospital."

An hour later, he was officially pronounced dead. The coroner's report said he died of a heart attack. I went to the hospital. I didn't believe it, and I had to see it for myself. Besides, after all the psycho movies I'd seen, it didn't matter how many times they got killed — they always came back to life!

The head nurse put her hand on my shoulder sympathetically. "He was too old, it was too big of an heart attack, and we couldn't revive him," she said.

Since I couldn't think of a politically correct way to say it, I replied, "George tried to kill me today. I came over to see if he was really dead."

"Yes, he is. He's at the mortuary," she informed me.

I went home and called the mortuary.

"Yes, he's really dead," the mortician said.

Two days later I was raking leaves in front of George's apartment. When I looked down the street, I couldn't believe my eyes! There was George's car, coming right toward me. I threw my rake in the air and ran in the house.

Completely out of breath, I said to my wife, "Crazy George is back! His car is headed this way."

She could see the fear in my eyes, but that didn't stop her from laughing as she said, "His friend came by earlier today to pick up his car."

Looking back, I believe George *wanted* to go to jail. He would have had someone to look after him, had free room and board, his meals provided, and all of his medical problems taken care of.

The friend that took his car confirmed this. "Because George was drunk and had lost it, you would have gotten shot, just because you were there," he said.

George could have taken a lot of things from me that day — all of my dreams, goals, and plans for the future. I've often wondered what life would have been like for my wife and son had the gun fired that day. I would have become Stoppable, and alcohol definitely would have played a major role in that. I'm relieved to say that the day I zigzagged, I was Unstoppable — and this saved me. Otherwise, I could have ended up a victim, just like **crabs in a bucket...**

Sometimes it takes an act of God
to "save" *The Unstoppable You!*

Lesson 24

Crabs in a Bucket

PEER PRESSURE IS A POWERFUL FORCE to be reckoned with, especially when you're a teenager. Almost all of my students have been affected by it, which is one of the reasons this story is among their favorites. Although short in length, it's long on lesson...

One day Tommy was walking to school. He met several of his friends along the way. They suggested to him that he skip school and hang out with them at the beach. Tommy knew he should go to school, but his friends easily convinced him to go with them.

Tommy had a blast that day, until he got home. When he walked in the house, his parents were in tears. Tommy's mom had gone to school to give him his lunch, which he had forgotten. When his teachers and mother couldn't find him, they called the police. Tommy's parents searched for him all day. His dad missed work. Now his parents were grateful he was alive. But when Tommy told them what he had done, he was thinking he was dead, or at least in deep trouble.

When Tommy's grandfather, Henry, got wind of the incident, he knew the time was perfect to take his grandson crabbing. Tommy always wanted to go, but his grandfather thought he was too young. Henry knew there was a valuable lesson to be learned from the crabs, and Tommy needed to learn it. They would go on Saturday.

Tommy was wide-eyed with excitement as he ran down the rickety weathered dock. He jumped into his grandfather's creaky wooden boat, then sat and watched his grandfather row out into the bay. Tommy listened to the rhythm of the oars squeaking in the oarlocks. He could smell the ocean in the gentle sea breeze and almost taste the salt. He observed intently as his grandpa showed him how to tie the bait on his string. Together, they dropped their lines into the bay.

"The weight will take the bait to the bottom," Grandpa explained. "That's where the crabs will eat it. Watch your line."

Magically, within minutes, Tommy saw his line twitching.

"You got one!" Grandpa yelled. "Pull him in."

As Tommy hauled in his hand line, Grandpa got the net ready.

"Not too fast, or he'll let go," he instructed.

With the crab several feet below the surface, Henry netted him. Tommy took the lid off the bucket and grandpa dropped the crab in. Immediately Henry put the lid back on. On this sunny day, the crabbing was good. Really good! They both caught a bunch. Eventually Tommy noticed that Grandpa had forgotten to put the lid back on the bucket.

"Grandpa, when there was only one crab, you put the lid on the bucket. Now that the bucket's half full, you don't use the lid anymore. Why?" Tommy asked.

"Because one crab can climb out of the bucket," explained Henry.

"Well, why can't they climb out now?" asked a confused Tommy.

At long last, this was the moment Grandpa had waited for. The lesson of the crabs.

"Watch the crabs," Henry said.

Tommy marveled at all the crabs in the bucket. There were so many he couldn't see the bottom. Watching closely, he noticed something intriguing. When one of the crabs would make it to the top of the bucket, another one would reach up and pull it back down. Over and over Tommy witnessed the crabs getting pulled back down in the bucket.

"Why do they do that?" he asked his grandfather.

"All of the crabs want out of the bucket," Henry began. "In their attempt to get out, they unknowingly pull the others back in."

Still watching closely, Tommy saw it was true.

"Tommy, sometimes our friends can be just like those crabs," Grandpa explained. "They may feel they're trapped in their bucket or a situation with no way out. The last thing they want to see is you getting out of the bucket. Misery loves company, Tommy."

It hit Tommy like a ton of bricks. Now he realized he had gotten pulled down in the bucket the day he skipped school. He made a vow to himself and his grandfather that it would never happen again.

As Grandpa rowed back to the dock, Tommy watched as one of the crabs got out of the bucket. It scurried about on the floor of the boat and Grandpa reached down and picked him up. Tommy watched as Grandpa seemed to look the crab right in the eyes, and he was nodding his head as he tossed the crab back into the bay.

Grandpa turned to a stunned Tommy and said, "He deserved it, he got out of the bucket."

All of the crabs that remained in the bucket got thrown into a boiling pot of water, and they were eaten. That's exactly what happened to one of my students — Don Smith. Only he's not called Don Smith anymore, he's referred to as **63934...**

Don't let the crabs pull you down.
Get out of the bucket so you can
become *The Unstoppable You!*

HE WASN'T ALWAYS A NUMBER. For the first nineteen years of his life, his name was Don Smith. He was a student of mine for three years. Although he wasn't one of the best woodworking students I've ever had, he never caused me a problem. But that all changed the night he became #63934.

Shortly after he left high school, Don stopped by our house one day. He needed a place to live, and wanted to rent an apartment. I had a policy never to rent to my students, but I made an exception for Don. To this day, I regret that decision.

I explained the rules to Don: no parties or underage drinking for obvious reasons. The last thing I needed was to have kids drinking on my property.

"Your first party will be your last one," I told him.

Little did I realize how prophetic that statement would be. He agreed, and all went well until the night of December 16.

A gentle snow was falling, and I was shoveling the sidewalk. I could hear a commotion coming from Don's apartment. I walked over and knocked on his door. A party was going on inside.

"Don, it's way too loud. I can hear you clear out to the street," I said as he opened his door.

When I looked inside, I could see everyone was drinking. I asked the one kid, "How old are you?"

"I'm eighteen. Who the bleep are you?" was his drunken response.

I told him who the bleep I was. I also told all of them to get their bleeping rears in bleeping gear and get the bleep out of there.

I watched as Don and his buddies walked through the snow after leaving his party. I was thinking about what I told him before he moved in. "Your first party will be your last." Tomorrow I would notify Don that he would need to find another place to live.

Tragically, before morning, Don would be living in another place — a place that no one would want to call home. And he'd be living there for a long, long time.

After Don and his buddies left the party, they drove to the convenience store and bought more beer. Then they went to the dance at the high school. They got kicked out of the dance when it was discovered that they had been drinking. They drove to the liquor store and got more beer.

Later that night, the party resumed again at Don's apartment. Luckily, I didn't hear it. I would have lost it on Don the second time, if I would have had to break the party up again.

Don's uncle, who he worked for, heard about the party. When the uncle showed up at Don's apartment that night, it was to get his son and take him home. Don and his uncle got into an argument.

His uncle's last words were, "I'm calling the police to report underage drinking!"

With his party busted up a second time, Don sat on his bed sulking. He hated his uncle for this, among other things. So, with the help of fifteen or so beers, Don walked to his uncle's home. He milled around a bush outside while his uncle lay watching TV inside. Those footprints around the bush would later incriminate Don.

"You had time to think," the police officer would later state at the trial.

Then Don kicked open the door and shot his forty-six-year-old uncle six times in the chest. He shot him with his .22 caliber rifle, and killed him.

Don was arrested later that morning. He was discovered walking less than two blocks from his apartment near Eighth and Rose Streets with a loaded .22 caliber rifle strapped to his back. His blood alcohol level was .15 one hour after his arrest.

The next day, police taped off his apartment as a crime scene. No one was allowed in. When they finally removed the tape, I entered his apartment. Don had a box of magazines in the kitchen, and he used that box as a target. He'd sit in his living room and practice shooting. Sometimes he missed the box, and there were bullet holes in the kitchen wall.

I found another box under his bed. This one was filled with photographs. I opened up a manila envelope. It had his class pictures from kindergarten through high school. I laid them in chronological order on his bed, staring at those pictures of an innocent grade schooler. "What happened," I thought, "that would take this innocent kid and turn him into a cold-blooded killer? What could I have done to stop this? What could anyone have done?"

I needed to talk with Don, so I planned to go to jail and visit him. I talked to him on the phone while looking at him through the glass window. He was crying.

We talked for awhile, and then I asked him the question, "Why did you do it?"

Don told me that his hatred toward his uncle had been brewing for a long, long time. He showed no remorse.

Less than a week later, Don sent me one of many letters. The first one was about **the dream...**

What a tragedy for the kids that get pulled back into the bucket. They will never get the chance to become *The Unstoppable You!*

Lesson 26

The Dream

SEVERAL DAYS AFTER I VISITED DON SMITH, my former student, in jail, I received this letter.

Mr. Conrad,

How's it going? Not bad here. My cousin never brought the drawing I was doing for you. But I have drawn a few here I can give you.

I had a dream you and I were fishing the river in one of my secret holes. We were catching little pike left and right. Then we both hooked a couple of monsters. It took quite a while to get them in. Yours was 56 inches and mine was 60 inches.

Then you and I wrote an article about the Yampa in the *In-Fishermen* magazine. Then Al Linder came to fish with us on his show and we all caught nice pike.

Are you still telling the Friday Stories? Here's something I wrote — thought you might like to use.

"I grew up in a life drug-infested, all these situations only once arrested. I saw people fall and rise, rise and fall. In this short life I've seen it all. So if you're not doing drugs, raise your hand. Because you will be rewarded life in the end." Well take it easy. I got to go.

> Your student
> and friend,
> *Don*

Ironically, later that summer I would get to live that dream. I took my Dad to Canada on a fishing trip. We just happened to be at the same lodge where the television crew from *Fishing North America* was filming a show.

The producer of the series wasn't having much luck that week. On the fifth day of filming, he invited us to go along with them. We had been catching big pike the previous four days and they wanted to get some of it on film.

What an unbelievable day we had! Dad and I caught huge pike, the highlight of the show. Our unorthodox method was then emulated by the producer, and he caught the biggest pike of his life! He then thanked us on national television.

It was off the charts!

When I got back home, our local newspaper asked me to write an article about pike fishing on the Yampa River. During this same time, Don Smith sat in his cell alone.

Then he went to trial. He was found guilty and sentenced to forty years without parole for killing his uncle. He was given a number, 63934, and sent to the maximum security prison in Cañon City. From there, he would send me ***letters from hell...***

The Unstoppable You prefers to live the dream!

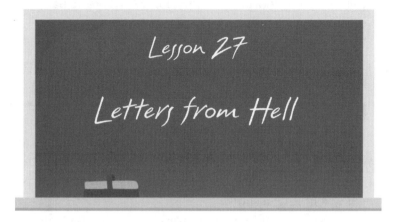

Lesson 27

Letters from Hell

THIS WAS THE FIRST LETTER DON SMITH, #63934, sent me shortly after being incarcerated at the Cañon City prison.

Mr. Conrad,

It was great to hear from you. I'm doing O.K. as I hope you are.

First off, as of now, I can't discuss the events of the night I was arrested. My case is still in the court system and my lawyer advised me not to discuss it right now.

However, I will tell you how it felt to be on trial. I think the trial was the most mind draining and stressful experience up until I came here. I couldn't understand all the legal mumbo jumbo discussed before, during and after the trial. My lawyers advised me not to speak on anything unless to them. I mean I was sitting quiet while the district attorney spoke lies and continually tried to make me look like a total ruthless individual. My life, my future was in the hands of 12 jurors and the judge. I had to hear a story I tried so hard to set aside. I had to look at very graphic photographs of the crime I so shamefully committed. I couldn't sleep at night, and when I did, fitfully. My future was out of my hands, as I so wanted some control. My lawyers kept trying to keep some confidence going, in my defense. The day I was sentenced, when the judge told me, "I have no choice but to sentence you to a life sentence," 40 years until I'm eligible for parole. If the state has their way, I won't be free again until 2030. All because I felt I needed to drink to have a good time. And in turn, the alcohol gave me the false confidence or false courage to take the life of another human being.

Now I sit in prison carrying the guilt and shame of being a convicted murderer. Here in prison, my crime is considered respectable. If it takes killing someone to get respect, I don't need it.

When I came to DOC [Deptartment of Corrections], I was scared to death. After seeing all the stereotypical events shown on TV — I mean, those things do happen here. Since I've been down, I've seen people stabbed, raped, thrown from the top tier. I've seen men hit with baseball bats, horseshoes, weights and locks stuffed in a sock. You have to fight, you have no choice. The weak are preyed upon here.

A week after I got to Shadow Mountain Correctional Facility, a man standing about 6'3" weighing probably 230 pounds came into my cell and said I was going to be his "punk" — that he was going to sodomize me. I was scared to death. I stood and told him he'd have to kill me. He took a step toward me and I kicked him in the shin with all I had. He grabbed his leg, and I kicked him in the other knee. As he hit the floor, I just kicked him and kicked. I then drug him out of my house [cell]. I stood shaking and trying to catch my breath. I couldn't believe it had been so easy. The man I defended myself from was a black man. Here in prison, racism is put right out in front. If you don't stand with your "white brother," you can't expect to be helped when you need help. If you don't have partners in prison, if you don't show that you'll stand with them, then you can't survive because they won't stand for you. Tattoos are a big thing here. People walk around exposing swastikas. White pride or black or brown pride written down the backs of their arms. I have friends who are totally covered with tattoos. When I was on the streets I really didn't know prejudice. But now that I'm in prison, I have no choice. I work alongside black people. But when it comes down to it, I'm expected to hate them.

One thing that all races are united on is the hate for the cops. Most cops are on the level, but there are those who continually disrespect you, treat you like a child, and there are those who are afraid to come out and say what they mean. They beat around the bush and lie to you. Another thing hated here is the sex offender, especially child molesters, and in my opinion they deserve no respect or consideration. Hate thrives here in the joint and it is expected.

Drugs and alcohol are here, too. You can get anything from homemade wine to marijuana to heroin here. It's all there to find on the yard. Drug debts, gambling debts and store debts are what causes most of the stabbings and fights here. People who run stores will sell you cigerettes, candy, food or whatever at prices which include 100% interest — one item for two with a week to pay. Every week you don't pay, it increases 100% until the store decides not to carry you. Then you take a beating or check in (go into protective custody). Which ranks down there with snitches and homosexuals.

Well that's about it for now. Getting late. I have to work tomorrow building electronic components for about three dollars a day. Until next time, take care.
Sincerely,
Don Smith #63934

I received several more letters from #63934 that year. I always wrote back. Eventually, I contacted the warden at the prison. I had an idea. I wanted all the kids at our school to hear Don's story — especially how the alcohol on the night of the shooting made him stoppable. The warden agreed it was a good idea. #63934 was going to tell his side of the story for the very first time. He would do it in front of a packed auditorium. Even the judge who sentenced him would be there. You could hear a pin drop as I dialed the numbers and made *the phone call...*

The choices we make can take us to heaven or hell.
The Unstoppable You makes the right choices!

Lesson 28

The Phone Call

MY PALMS WERE SWEATING AS I DIALED the number to The Department of Corrections in Cañon City. Over 700 students, parents, teachers, coaches, and administrators filled the seats in our auditorium. With the speakerphone hooked up to the PA system, you could clearly hear the dial tone and the ringing of the phone resonating through the air. It was electric! Over 700 people sat stone cold silent, anxiously waiting for the pickup at the other end...

As I looked into the eyes of the crowd, I thought about my former student, Don Smith, now #63934. I thought how alcohol made him stoppable. He certainly wasn't the first and, unfortunately, he wouldn't be the last. But his situation was the straw that broke my back. I'd had enough. It was time to do something, and this was it! I called the presentation *The Unstoppable You.* This was the very first one...

"Hello, Department of Corrections," rocked me from my daydream. It was showtime!

I first asked to speak with Don Smith's caseworker. The question I most wanted all of the kids to hear the answer to was, "How many inmates are in prison because of drugs and alcohol?"

"About ninety-five percent," the caseworker replied. "That is the national average as well."

After a few more questions, I asked to speak to Don. Everyone was on the edge of their seats. This was going to be the first time

Don would speak since the murder. His lawyer had him plead the Fifth Amendment at his trial. Even the judge who sentenced him was in attendance.

As soon as Don started to speak, it was obvious he was crying. He recalled sitting in that same auditorium only several years before. Now he was sitting in prison. He told the crowd how all his memories centered around high school. He didn't experience much after graduation, with the exception of the trial. He had dreamed of going into the military. But that dream had now become a nightmare!

I asked him to tell what happened the night he shot his uncle. Don explained in vivid detail the events leading up to the murder. He told how I broke up his party. He talked about going to the high school dance and getting more beer. He described walking to his uncle's trailer house and kicking open the door.

"Then I fired six rounds into his body," Don said in a cold, calculating tone.

When I asked Don how many of his friends who had been at his party had called, written, or visited him, he sheepishly replied, "None."

He also told of the fears he lives with every single day. He told about how one of his fellow inmates, a friend, was stabbed repeatedly in the neck with a screwdriver. That friend was partially paralyzed from the attack.

The crowd was visually moved when I asked him what he missed most.

"I miss walking on green grass. I miss seeing the moon and the stars. I miss going to the refrigerator and getting something to eat."

At the conclusion of our conversation, Don gave powerful advice, filled with sorrow and regret, for not following in his footsteps. I could see many eyes being wiped in the audience.

When I hung up the phone, the judge who sentenced him got up to speak. She explained why she gave Don forty years with no chance of parole. She also talked about his blood alcohol level the night of the shooting and the role it played in her decision. Having the judge speak right after hearing Don's testimony from prison packed a powerful one-two punch. It was unforgettable! The best part of it was when over ninty-five percent of the students shook my hand, making a commitment to be Unstoppable (drug and alcohol free.)

I would do many more phone conversations with Don in Colorado and Wyoming over the next several years. *The Unstoppable You* program always concluded with the overwhelming majority of kids making a commitment to be Unstoppable. I have personally shaken the hands of close to 100,000 kids as of this writing.

I still continue to do the phone call conversation as part of *The Unstoppable You* program. Only now, I make the phone call to a different number. Unbelievably, he's another former student. Even more unbelievably, he was in the auditorium when Don Smith spoke. He shook my hand and made a commitment to be Unstoppable. His name is Clint Haskins. Neither one of us could have ever imagined that someday he would become #21583 and had become **Stoppable...**

When the phone rings, make sure you're on the end of the line that is *The Unstoppable You.*

Lesson 29

Stoppable

IF I HAD TO LIST THE NAMES of the top ten students I've taught, Clint Haskins would definitely be on that list. He was reared by honest, hardworking ranching parents from Maybell, Colorado. They instilled some old-fashioned values in Clint — the kind of values missing from too many kids these days. Clint would always respond to my questions with, "Yes sir, Mr. Conrad." The kids called him a rancher, but Clint was more than that. He was a football player, wrestler, homecoming royalty, and a member of the rodeo team. Clint Haskins was the all-American boy. That's why I was shocked and stunned when I heard he was involved in the worst traffic accident in Wyoming history.

One day during Clint's freshman year, the electric garage door to my wood shop failed to close completely. The door remained open all night, and the next morning it was very evident that we had had a visitor — a skunk. The door was fixed that morning and I figured our problem was over. I was wrong. Over the next few days, the smell seemed to intensify. Finally, it became unbearable. The smell was coming from the plywood storage area. I had my students form a fire line to remove the wood and find the skunk. I needed someone to be first in line, and Clint immediately volunteered. After several minutes of handing wood back to his classmates, I heard Clint yell.

"I see it, I see it!" he screamed as he came charging out of the plywood room.

All of his other classmates scattered, running for their lives. We closed the door and called the animal control officer to remove the skunk. She arrived with a ten-foot rod with a hypodermic needle on one end. The skunk was about to get a lethal injection when the officer just started laughing.

"This skunk is already dead," she said.

The whole class busted up laughing, pointing at Clint. I nicknamed him "Sir Skunky."

When my son, Colton, was in second grade, he thought he wanted to be a cowboy. Clint was a junior in high school when he volunteered to teach Colton how to rope. What a sight the two of them were together in their cowboy hats! Colton barely stood waist high next to Clint, even with his cowboy hat on. Clint showed him how to throw a lasso at a fake steer head stuck into a bale of hay. Colton thought the time they spent roping was the "coolest thing on earth."

During Clint's senior year, he volunteered to be an elf at our annual Christmas event, called Santa's Wood Shop. Clint and his classmates spent two months building wooden toys for needy children in our town. The night of the big event, the children were invited up to our shop, which we had decorated like the North Pole. Santa and Mrs. Claus were there. The choir sang Christmas carols. There were cookies and punch for the little kids. We even broke open a couple of piñatas.

Next it was time for my students, who were dressed like elves, to give away the wooden toys they'd made. Clint's toy caused a huge commotion that night. He had made a rocking motorcycle and had his friend custom airbrush designs and flames all over it. Well, every little kid wanted that motorcycle, even the girls. No one wanted the painted ponies, the scooter airplanes, or the rocking llamas. They all wanted Clint's motorcycle. One father requested his son get the motorcycle because he had named him Harley after the Harley-Davidson motorcycle. I don't remember the name of the little kid that got Clint's motorcycle, but I'll never forget how happy he was! That little kid was the envy of every kid at Santa's Wood Shop.

After the final Friday Story Clint's senior year, I issued his class the Five Year Challenge. I didn't want to see any of them for five years. I did this at the end of the school year as a way to force my students to look forward and not look back on "the good ol' days."

"Now it's time to go out and accomplish something in the real world," I challenged. "Come back in five years and brag about what you've done."

Clint took this to heart. I didn't see him for nearly four years. Occasionally I'd see his mom, Lynn, around town.

"Clint hasn't forgotten your challenge," she'd say each time. "He's going to come and see you when the five year challenge is over."

Tragically, I would see Clint before the five years was up. The next time I saw him, he was dressed in an orange jumpsuit with his legs shackled together and his arms chained to his waist. He was being led by a police officer into the Albany County Courthouse. Clint was the soul survivor of the worst traffic accident in the history of Wyoming. He was accused of causing a head-on drunken driving collision that killed eight fellow student athletes from the University of Wyoming. With two-thirds of the cross-country team gone, the university had to cancel the rest of the meets for the season.

Still wearing the scars of the accident, Clint walked past me in the hallway outside the courtroom. I was about to walk into that same courtroom and face the families of the eight dead University of Wyoming cross-country student athletes. This would be the hardest thing I ever had to do in my entire life.

I could hear many of the family members sobbing as soon as I entered the courtroom. Clint's family was sobbing, too. This was Clint's bond hearing, and I was asked by his lawyer to speak on Clint's behalf.

On the night of September 16, just five days after the 9/11 tragedy, Clint Haskins drove his one-ton pickup truck from Laramie, Wyoming, to Fort Collins, Colorado. Clint had been drinking that night. Following a phone call with his girlfriend, he headed south to see her on Highway 287, one of the deadliest roadways in the country. Near the six-building town called Tie-Siding, police reports stated Clint crossed the yellow line. The time was 1:30 a.m. Heading north on the same highway was a Jeep Wagoneer crammed with the eight University of Wyoming cross-country runners. The two vehicles met head on. Clint's blood alcohol level was .16: the legal limit is .10.

As I took the stand in the courtroom, I was wondering what was going through the minds of the eight families. They had all experienced unbelievable grief and loss. Now I was going to speak about the character of the person they all believed killed their sons. To say I was nervous was an understatement.

Clint's attorney questioned me first. I was asked to relate things about Clint's character. Since he was my student for four years, I had many good things to say. When I spoke about Clint and Santa's Wood Shop, Clint started crying uncontrollably. So was everyone else in the courtroom.

When I finished, the prosecuting attorney asked, "Did you know Clint had a drinking problem, Mr. Conrad?"

I remembered Clint made a commitment to be Unstoppable (drug and alcohol free) after hearing Don Smith's phone call when Clint was a freshman. He shook my hand at the conclusion of *The Unstoppable You* program. I told the court I was not aware of a drinking problem with Clint.

At that point, the prosecuting attorney showed evidence of a drinking problem. He told how Clint was arrested three times as an MIP — a minor in possession.

The attorney went on to say, "After both occasions, Mr. Haskins continued to drink after his arrest, and now eight people are dead."

Afterward, the district judge slapped the gavel down and said, "Bond is set for $100,000."

Clint was led out of the courtroom and back into jail. I could hear his chains dragging along the floor as he left, mixed in with the sounds of many different people crying.

The drive back home was two-and-a-half hours long. The whole way, I kept thinking what a tragedy it was for everyone involved. Had Clint not been drinking that night, the consequences would have been totally different. Now alcohol, once again, would make someone Stoppable. In this case, nine young men became Stoppable. Someday, I thought, Clint would get a second chance. Sadly, the eight cross-country kids never would. I knew I would never forget the sight and sound of seeing one of my top former students in chains. Clint had become Stoppable.

Since the judge set a cash bond of $100,000, his family would have to pay the entire amount for Clint to be free until his trial. Usually it's just a percentage, but not this time. One hundred thousand dollars is a lot of cash, and I knew Dale and Lynn Haskins would be hard pressed to come up with it. That would be hard for anyone!

I figured I probably wouldn't see Clint again, until the day he appeared at my classroom door like ***an apparition...***

Alcohol doesn't discriminate when stopping
The Unstoppable You.

Lesson 30

An Apparition

ONE FRIDAY, shortly after the emotionally draining experience of Clint's bond hearing, I needed to teach my students the lesson I learned there. My students needed to hear it, too.

I started that Friday Story by holding up a small pebble in front of the class.

"Have any of you ever thrown one of these into a lake?" I asked. Every student raised their hand. "What happened when you did that?" I questioned, as if not knowing the answer.

"It made a splash," one student yelled out.

I pointed the pebble right at him and said, "That's right."

After leading the class with several more questions, we determined that the size of the splash was in direct correlation to the size of the rock. The bigger the rock, the bigger the splash. The smaller the rock, the smaller the splash.

"If you agree with this, raise your hand," I challenged.

Every hand in the class was raised. Some kids were looking at each other like, "Duh, everyone knows that." Some were wondering, "Where is he going with this?" They were about to find out...

"What happens next? What happens after the splash?" I asked.

Another student called out, "Ripples."

"Once again, you are correct," I exclaimed, getting more excited. I went on to explain that those ripples are caused by the displacement of water made by the rock.

"How far do those ripples go across the lake?" Now my questions were getting harder.

Not quite sure he had the right answer, one student answered sheepishly, "All the way across the whole lake."

That student was right. The ripples go clear across the entire lake. Obviously, you can't always detect them once they reach the other side, but they do go clear across. I explained to the class that their actions are kind of like that rock. Big actions create a big splash, small actions create a small splash. However, the size of the splash isn't nearly as significant as the ripple effect. Your actions of today will ripple out and can effect your life years from now, in a negative or positive way, depending on your splash.

I then told my class the story of Clint Haskins. He was one of the best kids I ever taught — polite, respectful, and athletic. He was the all-American boy. But Clint had three small splashes earlier in his life that had rippled clear across the lake and were affecting him now.

Those three small splashes were the MIPs (minor in possession) he was cited for and which were part of his record. At the time of the MIP, Clint had no idea that the ripple effect would play a major role in the judge's decision to set a cash bond at $100,000.

"How many of your parents have $100,000 in cash and could bail you out of jail?" Not a single hand was raised. "O.K. then, let's make sure the splash you create is a positive one so that the ripple effect helps to make you Unstoppable," I challenged.

Immediately after dismissing the class to go to work in the shop, I looked up and saw a figure at my classroom door. He appeared like an apparition — It was Clint Haskins!

With the small town support of family and friends, Dale and Lynn Haskins came up with the $100,000 in cash. Clint was free until his trial, and he came to talk with me. We went into my office. Clint was back in the very classroom where he spent four joyful and memorable years.

Our reunion quickly became emotional. Clint thanked me for taking the stand at his bond hearing. He told me he listened to every Friday Story during his four years, yet this still happened. I told Clint that nobody is perfect, including me. We all make mistakes. Why he was involved in such a tragedy, Lord only knows. We may never know why it happened.

Clint talked of the remorse he had for the eight cross-country kids — how he thought about them constantly, especially around the University of Wyoming campus. After his release from jail, Clint continued to take his classes at the same university that was deeply mourning the loss of eight beloved student athletes. I couldn't even imagine what he was going through, or the courage it took to go to those classes.

Eventually, the subject of his upcoming trial came up. Clint said there wasn't going to be a trial. When I asked him why, he said he wasn't going to put all those families through the emotions of a trial. He didn't want to put his family through it, either.

"I'm going to plead guilty," he said.

I told Clint that one thing no one can ever take from you is your character. "It sounds like you're keeping yours," I said.

On February 7, 2002, Clint took the stand during a fifteen-minute hearing. His attorney asked Clint if he was responsible for the head-on collision on September 16, 2001, that killed eight University of Wyoming cross-country athletes. Clint recalled the crash in tears.

While looking at all of the family members of the victims, Clint told them, "If I had not driven, they would still be alive."

Clint is currently serving a fourteen-to-twenty year prison sentence at the Wyoming State Penitentiary in Rawlins, Wyoming.

I went to visit Clint in prison. I will never forget all of the little kids I saw that day who were visiting their dads. It was there in prison that we discussed Clint becoming part of my program, *The Unstoppable You.* Clint wanted to try to make something positive come out of this tragedy. We agreed he would speak to students via a live phone call from prison.

It would take a second visit to prison to convince Clint to let the world hear *a message from Mom...*

Make sure your actions of today
cause a splash that will ripple out
and help create *The Unstoppable You.*

Lesson 31

A Message from Mom

THIS WAS GOING TO BE HUGE! It was definitely the biggest thing that ever happened at our school. After a dozen or more presentations at other schools, Clint would speak live from prison via telephone to his alma mater.

Clint speaking to over 700 students at his former high school attracted national media attention. Remember, it was in this same auditorium that Clint heard Don Smith's phone call when he was a freshman.

CBS's *The Early Show* would send two people from New York and two cameramen from Los Angeles to cover the event. The CBS affiliates would air this segment all across the country. Millions of people would see it.

Many of Clint's friends and family would be in the auditorium to hear Clint's live phone call from prison. However, what would take this presentation of *The Unstoppable You* off the charts was a message from his mom. Lynn Haskins would speak to the crowd, while Clint was listening on the phone.

I was granted permission from the Wyoming State Penitentiary to put together a video/slide show of Clint and the prison. I took my best friend and fellow teacher, Lance Scranton, along with me. Lance is 6'2" and weighs 250 pounds. He bench-presses 510 pounds. He played professional football in Canada for the Winnepeg Blue Bombers.

"Your job is to cover my back," I told Lance.

Halfway through our visit at the prison, I was thankful he was along. Although we were told we wouldn't come into direct contact with the inmates, we did.

It happened as two separate groups of inmates were coming and going to lunch. Lance and I were "trapped" between two sets of locked hallway doors. There were approximately thirty inmates and the two of us temporarily locked in that hallway together.

With no guards in sight, the inmates checked us over like "new fish," a term they use to describe fresh new inmates. Waiting for the doors to open was the longest five minutes of my life. Lance later told me he was praying the whole time.

Little did either one of us realize that that same hallway would be the site of a stabbing a few weeks later. The entire prison went into lockdown. Our phone call with Clint was canceled, and the CBS crew that was already in Colorado went back to New York. What a bummer! When the prison goes into lockdown, they interview every single inmate. This keeps the "source" of information anonymous. The process takes weeks, sometimes months. All we could do was wait. I figured the CBS crews from L.A. and New York would never come back to our little town the second time.

Unbelievably, after two weeks of lockdown, the crews returned. *The Unstoppable You* presentation was on again.

All of this was especially hard on Lynn Haskins. She wasn't really sure she wanted to do this from the beginning, and now it was getting harder. I made her a deal. Since no one knew she was going to speak that day, I would let her decide right up until the last minute if she would do it. She would let me know after Clint's phone call by nodding her head. I told her I would respect her decision either way.

Finally, on Friday, January 21, 2005, the much-anticipated presentation of *The Unstoppable You* was about to take place. The entire school was buzzing. Seeing Tracy Smith from *The Early Show* and the camera crews just added more anticipation and excitement. The day before this, Tracy Smith and the television crew interviewed Clint in prison. Now they wanted to get the reaction of the students listening to a former graduate. And what a reaction it was!

First, we played the movie that Lance and I put together from our visit to the prison. It was titled, *Stoppable!* with Clint Haskins. Featured were miles of razor wire and unforgettable images inside prison walls. When the movie ended, the only sound you could hear was the dial tone as I called the penitentiary.

As always, I talk first to Monte Thayer, the director of the In Reach-Outreach program at the prison. He answers my questions and tells the audience that ninety-five percent of all inmates are in prison because of drugs and alcohol. He also shares some Stoppable stories. He tells of one inmate who, at age thirteen, was scared to smoke dope. That same guy would later kill his best friend to get his pot. He used a hammer to crush his skull.

After speaking to Monte, Clint got on the phone. As soon as his voice came over the sound system, pictures of him from high school flashed across the movie screen, larger than life. His voice, along with the images, set off a cascade of emotions. While answering my questions, Clint told the sullen crowd about the first time he drank.

"I was a sophomore and was invited by the seniors to a high school party. Wanting to fit in, I went to the party and drank," Clint said.

He also spoke about the first time he made a decision to drink and drive.

"Some girls needed a ride home, and I didn't want to appear that I couldn't handle the situation, so I drove them home."

When Clint talked about the accident on September 16, 2001, his voice cracked with emotion. Pictures of the eight runners and the Jeep Wagoneer flashed up on the screen. It was gut wrenching!

He said, "There's not a day that goes by that I don't think about those eight guys and what I'm responsible for."

I asked Clint about the recent stabbing and lockdown incident. "What are some of the fears you live with everyday?" I asked.

Most of his fears were for his family — that something would happen to them, and he couldn't be there. One of his worst fears happened last year. Clint's grandfather died and Clint was unable to hug his grandmother at the funeral and tell her, "I love you."

Clint and I always end our phone conversation with his powerful testimony to accept my challenge to be Unstoppable (drug and alcohol free). He tells kids he once accepted that same challenge but did not take the commitment seriously enough.

"Seven years ago, I was sitting right where you are. You don't want to be where I'm at seven years from now," Clint told the crowd.

At that point, I glanced over at Lynn Haskins. This was her cue. Would she decide to speak? She was dealing with her own emotions this entire time. I couldn't believe it: she was nodding yes!

"Ladies and gentlemen, I have a very special guest here today, and she would like to talk to you. Please help me welcome Lynn Haskins, Clint's mom."

With Clint still on the phone listening, the cascade of emotions turned into a full-blown tsunami. Every single person was in tears — even my buddy, Lance. The television crews scrambled to get their microphones into position to receive this message from his mom.

I hugged Lynn as she walked on stage and whispered, "You can do this."

The only sound you could hear was hundreds of people sobbing. After adjusting the microphone for Lynn, she cleared her voice and said:

"This is real, and this can become a reality for any one of you. Bad things do happen to good people! Hello, my name is Lynn Haskins, Clint's mother. As Clint's mother, I could go on and on about his accomplishments, his kindness, and the quality person he is. However, you should know that in this situation, those things don't matter. It doesn't matter how good of a person you are. Making the choice to drink and drive can change you and your family's lives forever, as it has ours and the families of eight other wonderful young men. My dreams for Clint have turned to worries. I worry about his safety, about how the environment of a maximum security prison may change who he is and the future he will have. I worry that the twinkle in his eye may be gone forever, and the pain will never go away. And that the people who judge him so harshly can't see him for who he is and that he's not so different from their son, brother, or friend. Please don't let this happen to you and your family. I support what Mr. Conrad and Clint are doing, so I encourage you to take the challenge. Thank you."

As Lynn left the stage, over 700 people stood up and gave a heartfelt standing ovation. Clint heard it all on the other end of the line. More than 700 kids made a commitment that day to be Unstoppable! To date, that number is close to 100,000. Hopefully, they will keep the commitment they made, so they will never have to experience what my grandfather went through. For most of his life he was ***rough, tough, and hard to bluff...***

The Unstoppable You listens to Mom.

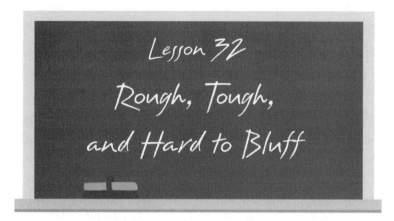

MY GRANDFATHER BUILT HIS OWN HOUSE. If that doesn't impress you, wait until you hear how he did it. He dug the foundation with a mule and a scoop. He foraged the fields for red sandstone rock. He would load the rock in a truck and drive back to the homesite.

One day, while driving an overloaded truck across the wooden bridge, the bridge collapsed. The rock spilled into the creek and the truck had to be pulled out. Once he got the rock home, he painstakingly chipped and cut each stone until it fit. Some of those stones weighed over 250 pounds. He did this for thirteen years.

I was always fascinated by the house my grandfather built. As one of several of his grandchildren, I frequently would ask questions like, "How did you lift those rocks so high?"

It seemed almost any question would elicit the same response, "'Cause I'm rough, tough, and hard to bluff."

It was Grandpop's favorite saying, and I always loved when he said it. I heard it a million times. Grandpop would brag that he graduated from the college of hard knocks. "Corn Cob University," he called it.

His degree was in hard, physical labor. He was a farmer, a stone mason, and an alcoholic. He started drinking at age thirty-four. He and the guy he worked with would occasionally stop at the bar after work. Eventually it became a habit, almost every night.

I really didn't know Grandpop was an alcoholic. However, I do remember going to the bar with him. He would load all seven of us grandkids in the back of his truck, its bed so rusted out that you could drop stones through it. We loved doing that and watching the stones fly down the road.

When we arrived at his favorite bar, he'd pick us up and put us on the bar stools. He would buy us each a Cola and a box of Cracker Jacks. His favorite beer was Pabst Blue Ribbon. After we all had a "few," we would race to the truck for the much anticipated ride home.

We grandkids would stand up in the bed of the truck and pound our little fists on the cab roof. This meant we wanted to go faster. Grandpop would go like a bat out of hell over Red Lane Road, which had a bunch of hills that would tickle our stomachs as we flew over them. Our moms would have had heart attacks if they would have seen it. It was better than any roller coaster ride! Just before we got home, Grandpop would go slow around the last corner, and we all sat down like we had been there the whole time.

One day, all seven of us were picking mint tea, which grew wild in the fields near our home. We noticed that the mean black Angus bull was chained in the meadow in a different spot, and figured someone moved him. We took off our jackets and waved them at the bull, pretending we were brave matadors, knowing the bull was chained. We even shouted, "Here bully, bully, bully."

Suddenly, my cousin screamed! We looked up and saw the bull charging right at us. We panicked and screamed and started to run. My brother, Kevin, tripped and fell. The bull lowered his horns as he closed in. Just at the last second, Kevin got up and scrambled over a log...where the bull stopped. It had busted his chain and nearly busted us. We ran for the one person we all knew was rough, tough, and hard to bluff...Grandpop.

I'll never forget how he walked up and twisted the ring in that bull's nose. The bull laid on his side, and we cheered and clapped. Grandpop really *was* rough, tough, and hard to bluff!

In high school, he only missed one of my basketball games my senior year. It just happened to be the most important one. We were playing one of our biggest rivals, Daniel Boone High School.

They were from the town of Birdsboro — the same town of Grandpop's favorite bar, Baselli's. Daniel Boone was undefeated.

A few days before the game, Grandpop fell and broke his arm. He was laid up from the fall and was going to miss the big game. Daniel Boone High School was heavily favored to win. Kevin visited Grandpop and told him we would win the game for him so that he could have bragging rights at Baselli's. The night of the game, my brother and I played inspired. Together, he and I scored thirty-nine points. We won 59-51! Grandpop had bragging rights for years!

One summer, after graduating from high school, I worked with my grandfather. My job was to take him to the bar after we checked out the job. He would show me what to do, and I'd pick him up at the end of the day. For this, he paid me a handsome sum, taking only beer money for himself.

Those are some of my fondest memories of my grandfather. Sadly, the one memory that I can't erase from my mind was watching him die. He weighed eighty-seven pounds and was wearing a diaper. He had lung cancer. In addition to drinking most of his life, he had also smoked since he was six years old.

His final wish was to leave the Reading Hospital and go home: he wanted to die in the house that he built. So they brought him home and hired a nurse to care for him. It didn't last long. Grandpop got worse and the nurse couldn't handle him. He died back in the hospital after all, hooked up to tubes and a ventilator. Rough, tough, and hard to *puff*. I watched Grandpop become Stoppable.

Watching him wither away and die is exactly what my students witness each year after hearing the Friday Story, **you are a banana...**

The Unstoppable You is rough, tough, and hard to bluff. Let's keep it that way!

Lesson 33

You Are a Banana

OF ALL THE FRIDAY STORIES, the one that lasts all year is You Are a Banana.

Newcomers to my classroom often comment, "Why do you have a banana hanging on your chalkboard? And why is it all black?"

I explain that the banana didn't look like that the first day I hung it there. It was green, so green you couldn't eat it.

"Over the next few days, something amazing is going to happen to this little green banana," I tell my classes.

While holding that little green Chiquita in the air, I question my students, "What's going to happen to the banana?"

They respond by saying, "It's going to get yellow."

I go on to explain they are correct, and over the next few days they will get to witness that. I then ask them what they want to do when the banana turns yellow.

"Eat it!" they yell.

"Smart class!" I fire back.

When the banana turns yellow, it means the banana is ripe. In fact, that's as good as it's going to get for the banana because that's when the banana is at its peak and when you want to eat it. Because if you don't eat it, then something else starts to take place. There's a split second of time when the banana quits getting ripe, and starts to rot. I don't know how to measure the precise moment that transition occurs, but there is a point in time where the banana quits getting better and starts getting worse.

"Class, you're going to witness it right before your very eyes," I exclaim. 'Cause this banana is going to hang here 'til the very last Friday of the school year."

"Sick," is their usual response.

"You and I are just like that banana. When we quit getting better — getting ripe — we start to rot. The banana doesn't have a choice. You and I do. We must continue our whole lives to commit to getting ripe. We never want to get completely ripe, because that means we can't get any better: we always want to be *getting* ripe, knowing that once we feel we can't get any better, smarter, stronger, healthier, et cetera, we start getting rotten."

The last week of school the banana is black, dried out, and as hard as a brick.

"Don't let this happen to you, my little Chiquitas," I tell my class.

"Keep getting ripe."

Only then will you be able to **conceive, believe, achieve...**

The Unstoppable You realizes that you're either getting ripe or getting rotten.

Lesson 34

Conceive, Believe, Achieve

ONE YEAR, I HAD MY PLANNING PERIOD the last hour of the day. Some days when I finished planning, I would head down to the weight room to work out. I just happened to be there one day while the PE class was doing its year-end testing. One of the tests was pull-ups and the teacher was recording how many each kid could do in her grade book.

When she called Debbie Gurr's name, Debbie said, "I can't do any."

The teacher put a zero in her grade book, then turned to me and said, "Her mother just passed away."

The teacher was using this as justification for not making Debbie try to do some pull-ups. At the same time one of my students, Jeff, turned and stared at me. He was in my class that very day and had just listened to the Friday Story, which was about using the word "can't." I call it "stinkin' thinkin'." I challenged my class that very day to never use the can't word.

"It's the worst four-letter word you can say," I told them. "It conditions you to be Stoppable."

Jeff never said a word when Debbie said, "I can't."

He didn't have to. I knew what he was thinking. I felt challenged. I walked over to Debbie to have a word with her. She told me she had never done a pull-up in her life. She even stuck both her arms out as proof. Standing barely 5 feet tall, Debbie was small

— even by high school standards — and her arms were thin. I told her to go off by herself and close her eyes.

"I want you to visualize yourself doing ten pull-ups."

She must have thought I was crazy. Toward the end of the class, I asked her if she did it.

"No," she said while trying to walk away from me.

I asked the PE teacher for permission to keep Debbie for a few minutes after class. Now it was just the two of us in the weight room. I began by telling her that I was very sorry to hear that her mom had passed away. Debbie had six brothers and sisters.

"I'm sure you all miss her a great deal," I said.

I know it's normal and healthy to mourn the loss of a loved one. But I was concerned that Debbie's mourning might prevent her from accepting challenges and taking risks. After all, Debbie was very much alive. Yet the PE teacher quickly accepted Debbie's "can't" and justified and excused it by Debbie's tremendous loss. To me, that was tragic.

After I explained that to Debbie, she showed me her arms again.

"Mr. Conrad, I can't do pull-ups. I've never done a single one in my entire life."

"Stop it, stop it right now!" I screamed. "I refuse to believe you can't do a pull-up! Your problem isn't your arms — your problem is right here!" I yelled while pointing at her head.

"You don't see yourself doing a pull-up, and until you can conceive it, then believe it, you're never going to achieve it! Now get over to the chin-up bar!"

Debbie was so small that she had to stand on a chair to reach it. I made her hold on to the bar and close her eyes.

"I want you to visualize yourself doing pull-ups on my count. When I say *up*, you see yourself pulling up. When I say *down*, you see yourself lowering back down."

I told Debbie I was going to count off ten pull-ups. She was to see herself doing all ten. When I finished counting ten, she was to open her eyes. I would keep counting, and she would do pull-ups for real. The poor girl was almost in tears from me yelling at her, but she nodded her head in agreement.

"Up Down One; Up Down Two!" I barked sounding like a drill sergeant. When I got to ten, I said, "Open your eyes."

"Up..." Debbie seemed to magically float over the bar.

"Down..." she let herself down.

"Up..." again her chin went over the bar.

"Down..." she started smiling.

"Up..." she almost got three.

At that point, her emotions erupted like a volcano. She was laughing and crying as she let go of the bar and hopped down off the chair. She gave me the biggest hug her tiny arms could muster.

"Thank you so much, Mr. Conrad," she said through the tears.

Then she ran up to the PE teacher and said, "Put me down for two and a half."

Through the years, I've told that story many times. The lesson of conceive, believe, and achieve is: Before you can achieve your goals, you have to first see it happening in your mind. Then you have to believe it (or, in Debbie's case, have someone screaming at you who believes it). Only then can you achieve it.

Our 2000 boy's varsity basketball team desperately needed that lesson. They were headed to the district tournament as the last place seed. Coach Blaine Corlett asked me to give the Bulldogs a pep talk before they left. Coach had asked four other times through the years, and the boys won after each talk. He was hoping this would be the fifth time.

As I told the team that story, I could see several of them wiping their eyes. They all realized they were "Team Debbie," and the district championship was their chin-up bar.

"You've got to see yourself beating those teams and holding that championship trophy over your heads. That's your chin-up, fellas," I said.

"Now, go get it done, Bulldogs."

At the district tournament, our boys shocked and surprised everyone. They crushed every team they played and won the championship trophy. Several of the players motioned for me to get in the team picture as they held that trophy over their heads. I didn't go, but I thought it was really cool that they invited me.

A couple of days later, the team requested that I come to practice. The guys had something they wanted to give me. When I arrived, Coach smiled and stopped practice, and the whole team gathered around me. The team's captain presented me with a shirt that read Bulldog District Champions on the front. But what really got me choked up was when they turned the shirt around. On the back of their championship shirts in huge bold letters, it read, "Conceive Believe Achieve, C. Conrad." I thanked the team and told them to always *be a big dawg...*

Whatever your pull-up in life is, you must *conceive* it, then *believe* it, so that you can go out and *achieve* it. That's what makes *The Unstoppable You.*

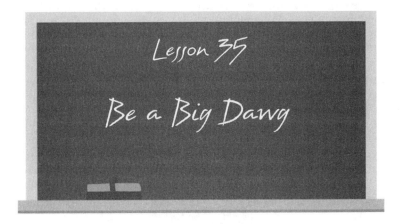

Lesson 35

Be a Big Dawg

THE MINUTE THAT SCRAWNY LITTLE FRESHMAN walked into the weight room, I knew what he was going to do. I watched as he and his friend put weights on the bar of the bench press. The scrawny freshman got into position to lift the weight as his friend spotted him. This was the moment of truth. After bragging and betting his friend about how much weight he could bench press, the time had come to prove it. I observed this scenario a thousand times.

The scrawny little freshman lifted the weight up off the bench rack with help from his spotter. Down went the weight as he lowered it to his chest. He pushed the weight back up, but only halfway before running out of gas. As the weight came back down, he asked his spotter for help. The spotter refused. Only after the scrawny freshman cried "uncle" did the spotter assist in helping him put the weight back up on the rack. The poor little scrawny freshman lost his bet. His friend razzed him as they left the weight room. I chuckled to myself, because I had seen it so many times before. Kids come and go from the weight room, never to return.

Amazingly the next day, the scrawny little freshman returned, this time without his friend. Even more amazingly, he kept coming back every day after school for four years. Unbelievable!

During those four years, I got to know that scrawny little freshman really well. His name was Kevin Rider. What I didn't know then was that I was about to witness this "little pup" meta-morphosing into a "big dawg."

On the day that "big dawg" came out of his dog house for good, he did so in front of a stadium full of fans, in the biggest game of his life...

Kevin took my class his senior year — not so much to learn woodworking, but to hear the lessons of the Friday Stories. One of Kevin's favorites was the story of Babe Ruth — a story as legendary as Babe himself.

It was the final game of the World Series, ninth inning, two outs, Yankees losing, and up to the plate steps Babe Ruth. After a couple of swings of the bat, Babe backed away from the plate and pointed his bat at the center field wall. He was telling all of the fans at Yankee stadium, the opposing team's pitcher, and the little kid in the hospital that that was where the ball was going. Most importantly, Babe was telling it to himself. He was thinking home run, not strikeout.

The crack of the bat was matched only by the roar of the crowd as Babe sent the ball over the center field wall. When Babe crossed home plate, he was mobbed and disappeared in a sea of humanity.

A reporter later congratulated him and asked, "What if you would have struck out?"

Babe replied, "The thought never even crossed my mind."

Babe wasn't worrying about striking out. He was focused on hitting a home run.

Kevin loved that story, because he was a baseball player. That's why he lifted weights after school everyday. During his final home game of his senior year, Kevin would put his strength to the biggest test of his life. He and his teammates were playing for the league championship that Saturday.

The Monday before the big game, Kevin wore a No Fear T-shirt to class. On the front of the it were two huge mean looking dogs. They had spiked collars and gnarled teeth. The back of the shirt read, "It's not the size of the dog in the fight, it's the size of the fight in the dog. No Fear." Immediately after seeing the shirt, I began teasing Kevin in front of the class.

I said, "Hey, Mr. Big Dawg — ruff, ruff! I'm just a little pup — yip, yip. But if I were a big dog like you — ruff, ruff — I'd take a bite out of that team you're playing Saturday for the championship — ruff, ruff."

Kevin laughed along with the rest of the class each time I barked. "Since I'm just a little pup — yip, yip — I could never do something like that," I said. More laughter came from the class. "I challenge you to be a big dawg on Saturday and do the Babe Ruth thing and hit a home run — ruff, ruff. On top of that, I'm inviting your entire class to come and see your home run on Saturday — ruff, ruff." Ol' Mr. Big Dawg tucked his tail between his legs and sat down. Although he was laughing, he didn't say a word.

That Saturday, I attended my first high school baseball game ever. I was seated on the third baseline behind home plate. It was a cool but sunny day. You could smell the fresh cut grass of the infield. This game was for the district championship and Kevin Rider's team — the Bulldogs — were playing against the Palisade Bulldogs. The game was billed as being a dogfight. I thought about Kevin's No Fear shirt. "It's not the size of the dog in the fight, it's the size of the fight in the dog."

Kevin's Bulldogs were down 3-1 in the bottom of the third inning, and they were at bat. There were two men on base with Kevin on deck. The batter at the plate was walked, and then the bases were loaded. Kevin stepped up to the plate as the crowd screamed, I offered my support and encouragement for him by "barking" at him. Yes, that's right. I was barking! I was barking to remind Kevin to be a big dawg.

Several fans made the comment, "Oh, that's the wood shop teacher; he's kinda crazy!"

The first pitch came in: a swing and a miss...strike one. The second pitch, a curve ball: another swing...strike two. Sensing my boy was in trouble, I started barking louder, "Ruff, ruff, ruff!" Those same people that thought I was crazy, started moving away from me. With two strikes on him, bases loaded, and me barking like an idiot, Kevin stepped back up to the plate after strike two. I can no longer recall what happened next. Kevin fought off the pitcher by hitting some fouls. The pitcher threw a couple of balls. Then, with the count 3-2, the bat cracked like lightening with a thunderous roar! I watched and will never forget as Kevin sent the ball over the left field wall. Home run! Grand slam home run! The stands were hopping, going nuts! The ball went clear out of the ballpark and rolled across the highway in front of some cars. Kevin's teammates ran out of the dugout. I stood on my feet barking and yelling like a child.

Kevin made sure his foot touched each bag as he rounded the bases. After he tagged third base and was headed home, he pointed to me in the stands as if to say, "That, little pup, is what a big dawg can do!"

Still on my feet, barking, with hands in the air, I gave Kevin a one-man wave, bowing down as he tagged home. Kevin was mobbed by his teammates, and — after our Bulldogs took the lead 5-3 — Palisade never scored again. Kevin's team won their first league championship in almost ten years.

That next Monday, back in the classroom, I congratulated Kevin in front of the entire class.

I asked, "Did you hear me barking?"

Kevin laughed, "Yes, I heard you barking."

"What was going through your mind at that moment?" I wanted to know. "What were you thinking with two strikes on you, the bases loaded, the game on the line, and me barking like a fool?" I asked.

Kevin answered, I was just thinking, "Hit the ball!"

Just like old Babe Ruth, he took his team to victory.

One of Kevin's classmates asked, "How did you know Kevin would hit a home run?"

I replied, "That was easy. That home run was destined to be hit the day that scrawny little freshman came to the weight room and STAYED!"

The lesson Kevin taught us all was ***don't quit...***

For the times in your life when you have to be a dog,
be a big dawg! That's *Unstoppable*!

THE BEST THING ABOUT TEACHING in the same school for over twenty-six years was seeing how my "projects" turned out. I referred to my students as my projects. Every Friday, I would work on those projects, and my favorite "tool" was the Friday Stories. The purpose of these stories was to "build up" the students.

Each year after the final Friday Story, I would tell my students, "It's up to you to finish the project that I started, and autograph it with excellence."

Rich Sadvar was one of my projects. He required a ton of work: in fact, I had to work overtime! The first day I met him, he threw stones at me — literally! I was working as a maintenance man after getting RIFed (reduction in force) from my teaching job. I was back in my former wood shop one day, cutting sheets of plywood. Rich was turned loose unsupervised in that shop.

When Rich threw a fistful of stones at a classmate, I got hit in the crossfire. I was furious! If someone would have told me that day that the same mischievous young man would, many years from now, become a physical therapist and treat my son, I would have said, "Impossible!"

As it turned out, I got my old teaching job back Rich's sophomore year. The second he walked into the classroom and saw the maintenance man he had hit with stones the year before, he knew things were going to be different. This self-confessed misguided youth just needed direction to channel his energy.

With some direction, Rich started to excel. He excelled not only in my class, but on the wrestling mat as well. I got to really liking this kid. We went hunting and fishing together and had a blast every time.

At the conclusion of his senior year, Rich confided in me that he was thinking about doing something no one from his entire family tree had ever done: he wanted to go to college. He wanted to become a wood shop teacher, "Just like you," Rich said.

I knew the road he was choosing was going to be tough, especially for Rich. So before he left for college, I gave him a hand written copy of the poem, *Don't Quit*, along with some money to help him out. This was the same poem my parents gave me when I was in high school. Rich read that poem for the first time before he left for college.

Don't Quit

When things go wrong as they sometimes will,
When the road you're trudging seems all uphill,
When the funds are low and the debts are high
And you want to smile, but you have to sigh,
When care is pressing you down a bit,
Rest, if you must, but don't you quit.
Life is queer with its twists and turns,
As everyone of us sometimes learns,
And many a failure turns about
When he might have won had he stuck it out;
Don't give up though the pace seems slow —
You may succeed with another blow.
Success is failure turned inside out —
The silver tint of the clouds of doubt,
And you never can tell how close you are,
It may be near when it seems so far;
So stick to the fight when you're hardest hit —
It's when things seem worst that you must not quit.

— Anonymous

While Rich was at college he met Nancy, a big-city girl addicted to the mall. She was fun loving and high spirited, just like Rich. My wife and I asked Rich and Nancy to come with us to see Hank Williams, Jr. in concert. During the middle of the performance, Rich asked Nancy to marry him. She said yes. I couldn't believe it! My rowdy friend was settling down, as ol' Hank would say.

Not long after the wedding, they had a son. Now, in addition to raising his level of education, Rich had to raise a family. He read the poem a second time. While his wife worked as a dental hygienist, cleaning every tooth in Laramie, Rich attended classes.

After five years of college, and just three months from graduation, Rich told Nancy, "I don't want to be a teacher, I want to be a physical therapist."

That meant another four years of college. That day, Nancy told Rich she was pregnant again. This time they both read the poem together. They struggled to survive — I mean *really* struggled. Many times, when Rich felt like giving up, he'd read that poem again and again. It gave him strength and hope.

After nine years of college in his head and a tattered and worn out copy of the poem in his hand, Rich finally graduated from college. He gave that worn and tattered copy to his mom, Paula. At age forty-two, she used that same poem as inspiration to help her get her GED.

On January 10, 2004, Rich returned to the same wood shop where he hit me with the stones. He was a live Friday Story, only this time he wasn't throwing stones: he was throwing words of advice.

"Don't quit," Rich told the kids. "Amazing things can happen when you don't quit. I still have my original copy of the poem that Mr. Conrad gave me. It's in my orthopedic physical therapy clinic now."

Each kid received a copy of the poem that day.

In the spring of 2006, Rich became the head baseball coach at his high school alma mater. He instilled that don't-quit attitude in his players, and the team went undefeated and won the league championship his first year as head coach. He was named coach of the year, an honor he received two years in a row! No other baseball coach in our school's history has ever accomplished that. Amazing things really *do* happen when you don't quit!

Rich also taught his players to **bundle up and stick together...**

The Unstoppable You doesn't quit, ever!

Author's note: Although I'm a firm believer in the don't quit attitude, there are certain situations that are toxic, abusive, or dangerous to your emotional or physical wellbeing. If you find yourself in one of those situations with your relationships — boss, coworkers, coach, teammates, etc. — the best thing you can do is get out of that situation (bucket) and move forward in a positive direction.

I WAS HONORED TO GIVE the commencement address at Montrose High School on Memorial Day weekend in 2006. I immediately got the attention of approximately 2,500 people when I called Ashley and Tyler to the podium.

Ashley was the smallest girl in her senior class. Tyler was one of the biggest and strongest athletes in the same class. As the two of them made their way to the podium, I got out my bundle of wooden sticks. I handed Ashley one of the sticks and asked her to break it...she did so, easily. The crowd cheered. I then handed the bundle to Tyler with the same instructions.

"Break it," I said.

The harder Tyler tried to break the bundle, the louder the crowd cheered as the cheer eventually grew into a roar, an exhausted Tyler finally proclaimed, "I can't break it; it's impossible."

I thanked Tyler for *not* breaking the bundle.

"'Cause you would have ruined the rest of the story," I chuckled.

The crowd laughed.

I then proceeded to explain the *wisdom of the wood,* as I like to call it. This wisdom applies to your school, your family, your team, or your business. The lesson becomes obvious when you replace the pieces of wood with people. One by one we are easily broken, but if we bundle up and stick together, we are unbreakable.

I thanked the two seniors for helping demonstrate that fact. As they took their seats, I shared a real life example from the *wisdom of the wood*. I told the crowd what occurred in the Fall of 2005 in my son's **second hour class...**

One by one, we are easily broken, but if we bundle up and stick together, we are unbreakable and *Unstoppable*.

Lesson 38

Second Hour Class

ONE MORNING, THE KIDS IN MY SON'S second hour class rose and began to recite the Pledge of Allegiance. My son, Colton, who was a sophmore, heard Armando say, "I pledge allegiance to Mexico." Armando sat down.

Colton said to Armando, "Stand up and show some respect."

Armando told Colton to shut up and called him a name that, let's just say, wasn't Mother Goose. Colton fired back by calling Armando a name that wasn't Richard Head. Both of them got sent to the dean's office. Now, are you ready for this? You better sit down.

Colton and Armando were both charged with sexual harassment. Personally, I didn't care that they were both sent to the office. But — sexual harassment? Come on; let's get real! That's another example of political correctness run amuck — which is when I got involved.

When I questioned the sexual harassment charge, I was told that Armando used the 'F' word. Since both of them were responsible for disturbing the class, the teacher who sent them to the office said, "I couldn't charge one and not the other."

I called the charges ludicrous and ridiculous. "No way should a kid be charged with sexual harassment for having the courage to tell someone to show respect for the American flag," I demanded.

"Furthermore, as Colton's father, I can assure you we will not be pressing charges on Armando for dropping the 'F' bomb."

I was livid. I demanded they drop the charges on Colton and Armando and the foolish political correctness. Needless to say, they dropped the charges. I also said I wished the teacher would have handled it in a different way.

"Well, what would you have done?" they asked me. So, I proceeded to tell them what I *did*...

Armando was in my last hour class. I walked up to him fifteen minutes after class started and said, "I understand you and Colton got into it today."

Armando hung his head and shook it while shamefully saying, "Yeah."

"Do you know why?" I asked.

Armando said, "Because of the Pledge of Allegiance."

"Yes," I said. "But, do you know *why*?"

Armando shook his head no.

"Would you like to know?" I asked.

Armando nodded yes.

As we walked into the classroom away from the noise of the wood shop, I asked Armando if he had any brothers or sisters.

"I got me two sisters," he said in broken English.

I told Armando that was cool, and that Colton had no brothers or sisters. He's an only child. Or he was, until Chance Phelps moved into the apartment next door...

Chance was a seventh grader, Colton was a second grader, and they adopted each other as brothers. Many times Colton and Chance tossed the football and baseball in the yard. Chance would invite Colton over to play Nintendo. When Chance's seventh grade buddies came over, he didn't ask Colton to leave because his real friends were there. He would always include Colton, his "little brother."

I said to Armando, "How cool is that — a seventh grader hanging out with a second grader?"

"That's pretty cool," Armando remarked.

I explained to Armando how Chance lived next door for two years. He took wood shop in high school and was a "Brother

Woods" — a title earned by displaying a tradition of excellence in the wood shop. Chance had many friends because of his personality. When he was a junior, his mother moved to Palisade, and Chance graduated from Palisade High School. He was still a Bulldog, but one of a different color.

As Armando listened intently, I went on to explain how Chance got a "job" right out of high school. One day at his "job," he volunteered to do something that not a lot of others in his profession liked to do — man the .50 caliber machine gun in the turret of the lead Humvee in a convoy that was ambushed in Iraq.

"Knowing the kind of boy he was, I can only imagine the kind of Marine he became," I told Armando.

Chance volunteered to be the machine gunner, knowing full well that that made him a target for the enemy.

"Well, Armando, the enemy shot that day, and Chance reportedly returned fire, covering the convoy until he was fatally wounded. He came home in this box," I said while turning the page of the Brother Woods scrapbook. I pointed to the coffin that Chance came home in. He was only nineteen years old. An entire page of the scrapbook is dedicated to him. On that page are images ranging from high school football to the horse drawn carriage that carried Chance to his grave. I asked Armando if he could see what was draped on top of the coffin.

A teary-eyed Armando replied, "The American flag."

"In that coffin is Colton's big brother," I quietly said to Armando.

I then paused for a few moments before telling Armando how a couple of Marines would fold that flag and give it to Chance's mother, Gretchen.

I watched as a single tear rolled down Armando's cheek. "I'm sorry Mr. Conrad. I pledge tomorrow," Armando said while wiping his eyes.

"No, Armando, I didn't tell you this story to force you to say the Pledge. I shared it with you so you could understand where Colton is coming from."

I patted Armando on the back while asking if he remembered the lesson Bundle Up and Stick Together. Armando nodded yes. "When you sit down during the Pledge of Allegiance," I told Armando, "you break some of the sticks in the bundle — 'cause you have classmates who have brothers and sisters, and a few have their fathers over there, fighting for our freedom from terrorists. They're fighting for the very freedom you benefit from, living in this country."

I concluded our conversation by informing Armando that the only reason he can sit down, if he chooses to, is because of the ultimate sacrifice people like Chance made. I simply asked Armando to remember that the next time he said the words *I pledge allegiance...*

Some of life's best *Unstoppable* lessons occur outside of the second hour classroom.

Lesson 39

I Pledge Allegiance...

I KNEW WHAT THE FRIDAY STORY had to be that week, because of the incident that happened during the second hour class involving Colton and Armando. I decided to recite the Pledge of Allegiance. I wanted to explain its full meaning to all of my classes. Little did I realize that Friday that I would later recite my interpretation of the pledge in front of 2,500 people. It was at Montrose High School's graduation on Memorial Day weekend. I was interrupted three times as the crowd cheered when I told them the same Friday Story that I told my class...

I pledge allegiance to the flag of the United States of America... I questioned my first hour class, "What does 'allegiance' mean?" Unbelievably, no one knew.

"O.K.," I said. "Your Bulldog football team is playing the Steamboat Springs Sailors. Who are you cheering for?"

"Bulldogs!" the class shouted in unison.

"That's what allegiance is," I explained. "It's devotion to a person, cause or — in this case — a country. It's who you are cheering for." I raised my voice when I told the class to notice, "It says the United States of America, not the divided states of America."

And to the Republic for which it stands... "A republic is a form of government. In the United States, it's a government of the people, by the people, for the people. It's not about the politicians in Washington.

"The politicians make me so mad, there are days I don't feel like doing the Pledge," I told my class. "However, I pledge to honor the ultimate sacrifice people like Chance Phelps made. He was one of the many who paid with his own life for us to be free."

One nation... In addition to my class, I told the crowd at Montrose High School, "You're not an Irish-American. You're not an Italian-American. You're not a Japanese-American. If you are a legal citizen of this country, you are an American. Drop the other nationality. It only splits the bundle."

Over 2,500 people at Montrose's graduation went nuts! They started clapping and whistling and didn't stop! I walked to the back of the stage and got a drink of water. When I returned to the podium, they were still cheering!

Under God... "Oops," I covered my mouth with my hand. "I said the G-word; said it in a public place. I guess the ACLU will be after me now. Don't laugh, it's happened to others. There are forces in this country that want to remove God from the Pledge of Allegiance, take God off the back of the dollar bill, and eliminate God from all public buildings — and not to mention take away the nativity scene at Christmas. Here's a little statistic for you, if you don't believe this country has been blessed by God. Ninety percent of the world's population doesn't even own a car. They live in poverty, by U.S. standards. One thing that cannot be denied: this country was founded and based on a belief in God. God, please continue to bless America," I said. For the second time, the crowd went wild.

Indivisible... "This country tried it once. We called it the Civil War. We were divided: the North had its own flag and its own money. The South had the Confederate flag and Confederate money. Brother fought against brother as a divided nation fought with itself. Not far from my childhood home in Pennsylvania was the Battle of Gettysburg. Over 50,000 Americans died in those fields. Some of the creeks ran red for days with the blood of Civil War soldiers.

"If you ever get the chance to go see the battlefield, do it," I challenged the kids in my class and the crowd at graduation. "The battlefield has been preserved to be just like it was during the Civil War. You will literally be transformed to another place and time.

"Most unforgettable for me personally was what I saw in the museum. In addition to all of the artifacts and relics, they found many bullets. Shockingly, many of those bullets hit head-on. Americans from the North shot at Americans from the South, and their bullets hit in midair. What are the chances of that? It is a gut-wrenching example of how divided this country once was. We must never go back.

"Ironically, having said that, when I was in first grade, the alarm would ring and the teacher would lock the door and turn off the lights. All of us kids would hide under our desks. Who were we hiding from? We were hiding from the USSR, and the fear of the Cold War was anything but cold. Sadly, since the tragedy at Columbine High School, the alarm will ring at our school. The teachers lock the doors and turn off the lights. All of the kids hide, but we are not hiding from the Russians anymore. We are hiding from each other. Kinda scary!"

With liberty and justice for all... "We haven't always gotten that right in our country. Just ask the Indians — ask the Blacks. But I believe we got it right, now. As I write this, the United States is building a fence on our border with Mexico. That fence isn't to keep Americans in the United States: it's to keep the illegal aliens out. People coming from Cuba float on inner tubes across shark-infested waters just to get into our country.

"Mexicans by the millions come here illegally. In fact, just last year, I heard a story about a cleaning lady working in California who went back to Mexico to visit her sick mother. She got back into our country by being stuffed inside the car seat. In other words, she was the stuffing! A big part of the reason they come here is because the average daily wage in Mexico is under $5. America is still the land of milk and honey; I believe it's the greatest country in the world!"

I then challenged the kids in my class, and also the graduating class at Montrose High School, to make sure they help "keep it that way." So you can imagine their reaction when I introduced them to one of my former students.

"He helped keep it that way!" I exclaimed! "He is **the ?*!#*ing Mexican...**"

Hopefully we will continue to be one nation under
God, indivisible, with liberty and justice for all.
That's what makes this country *Unstoppable*!

Lesson 40

The *?#!*ing Mexican

FOR SEVERAL YEARS I COACHED BASKETBALL at the high school where I taught. I was in the coach's office in the varsity locker room one day, when Marc Juarez knocked on the door.

"Coach, can I talk to you?"

"Sure, come on in," I said.

Once inside and after closing the door, Marc told me he was having a problem at school.

"What's the problem?" I asked.

Marc told me the kids were calling him a *?#!*ing Mexican. Initially I laughed, because I thought he was joking. He wasn't joking. I remember thinking who would be stupid enough to call him any name besides Mr. Juarez. Marc was the varsity heavyweight wrestler on a state championship team. Although he was a heavyweight, he wasn't fat. He was just big and muscular.

"Who's calling you that, Marc?" I asked.

"Oh, kids in general and members of my wrestling team," he said. "Coach, what do I do?"

Since he was looking for advice, I simply told him how I felt the Marc Juarez that I knew would handle this. Both of us were well aware of the trouble he'd get into if he beat them up, especially the smaller kids.

"The Marc Juarez I know will find them when they're alone, one on one. You will get your nose this far away from theirs," I held my thumb and index finger one inch apart, "and tell them in no uncertain terms that you better never hear that garbage coming out of their mouth again. 'Cause if I do, you and I will meet again, my friend. And you will lose.'" Marc nodded his head in approval.

"I also have a problem when I go into certain stores in Denver. The store owner follows me around. What should I do about that?" Marc questioned.

I challenged Marc to put himself in the store owner's shoes. I explained to him that the store owner had possibly been stolen from in the past.

"Whether it was kids of your race, or kids of your age — you have two choices," I said. I told Marc he could reinforce that store owner's stereotype or he could break it by being the kind of person we both knew he was.

Marc thanked me for the advice and left. I would never have imagined that one day he would give this advice to the most powerful person on the planet — the President of the United States of America.

Marc graduated in the Spring of 1997. I didn't see or hear from him until the Winter of 2002, when I was honored to run with the Olympic Torch in Aspen, Colorado. It was awesome! I was nominated by the local Chevrolet dealership as someone who inspired others. Marc saw the picture of me carrying the torch on the internet, and he emailed me this letter. I've read it many times, sometimes to groups as small as fifteen to twenty. Sometimes I've read it to thousands, and the reaction is always the same...

Mr. Conrad,

Great picture in the paper. I usually scroll through the *Craig Daily Press* over the internet. That must have been motivating, carrying the Olympic Torch.

I hope you're still doing your lessons and lectures on drugs and alcohol. This nation could use more teachers like you. I apologize for the email being a little choppy. I'm somewhat in a rush. *[You'll find out why he's in a rush in a minute.]*

I wanted to email you and encourage you not to stop with your program *[The Unstoppable You]* and keep pushing to keep students on track. I still remember a lot of your parables and usually mention them to my Marines when they come across trouble. The most common one I tell is the one where the crab in the bucket keeps trying to climb out but all his little buddies keep dragging him back down.

Unfortunately, my brother didn't have the will power to pull himself out of the bucket. I learned about three weeks ago that my brother is facing prison time, up to two years, for drug trafficking from Mexico to the U.S. He just wanted to make that quick cash and eventually it all caught up to him.

His lawyer contacted me and asked me if I would take responsibility as a big brother and bail him out 'til he goes to court. He was trying to make me feel guilty and make a little money by me posting his bail and paying his lawyer fees. Well, I didn't want to hear he was in jail, let alone let him stay there, but as a big brother I told his lawyer he can stay there in jail and pay his own dues, 'cause if he's going to be drug dealing, who knows how far he has infected other families and how many families he has destroyed. So I made the decision not to assist him. My mother is in Mexico enjoying herself, so I was the only relation that could get him out.

For the first few nights, I was upset about my decision but, then again, I reckoned that's why they call it "tough love." He may be mad at me, but at least he'll be alive and mad at me versus being dead and me wondering whether I could have helped him. *[Hear what he did? He let his own brother stay in jail because he cares more about our society!]*

> As far as I go, I'm in preparations to go overseas and be a part of Operation Enduring Freedom. I was at New York after the aftermath *[of 9/11]* scoping out possible bombs, evacuating people from homes, and trying to prevent rioting.
>
> It makes me proud to be doing what I do and getting ready to "bear arms." It is people like you that motivate me to be a part of this war in keeping the terrorists away so that your way of life, the nation's way of life, can remain.
>
> God speed and again congrats with the torch,
> Marc Juarez.

When I finish reading his letter, I always conclude by saying, "The ?*#!*ing Mexican." I tell my students, "So, before you get ready to spew that garbage out of your mouth — think! Someday that person could be protecting your very own way of life! Instead of spewing your garbage, maybe you should say thanks."

That's exactly what I sent back to Marc via email.

The next time I saw him was in the Spring of 2006. I asked him for a quick update since his email. Wait to you hear the rest of his story...

Marc was at Ground Zero after the 9/11 tragedy. It was October, and it was cold that night. He was warming himself by a fire burning inside a fifty-five gallon drum. A limousine pulled up. Inside was Mayor Rudolph Giuliani and President George W. Bush. The President invited Marc to dinner at the Governor's mansion. Marc thought there would be hundreds of others invited. When he got there, he was amazed! There were not hundreds of others present: It was him, two fellow Marines, Mayor Giuliani, and President Bush. That's it, along with a few Secret Service men.

President Bush told Sergeant Marc Juarez, "The weight of the world is going to be resting on our shoulders for the next few years." The President then pointed his finger at Marc and asked, "What do you think we should do?"

Sergeant Marc Juarez told the President of the United States of America, "Mr. President, if you say, "Go!," my Marines are ready!"

WOW!

Marc was sent to Afghanistan as part of an elite Marine force to capture Osama bin Laden. He estimated his troops were within half a day of capturing bin Laden at one time. They took sticks and stirred through his feces. They could tell what he'd been eating and the condition of his health.

At one point in the pursuit of bin Laden, Sergeant Juarez sent part of his convoy through a field to make sure it was clear. He received a thumbs-up from his radio man. Marc took several steps into the field when he caught a glimpse of motion off to his left side. A Taliban soldier attacked him. Remembering his old high school wrestling moves, Marc instinctively got him in a head lock. As he spun him to the left, Marc shot his attacker in the head with the 9 mm pistol he had strapped to his chest. He fired again when they hit the ground. Both shots were fired without Marc removing his 9 mm from its holster. He fired right through it.

When members of his troop rushed over, they found Marc covered in blood. They didn't know if he'd been shot or not. When they went to remove his flak jacket, Marc passed out. He had been stabbed and the removal of the jacket buried the knife deeper. The pain was intense. The rusted knife was left in Marc's lower abdomen for two hours, since removing it would have caused him to bleed to death. They were in the middle of nowhere in Afghanistan. A helicopter was called in to rescue Marc. As he was being airlifted, he held on to the rope with both hands in excruciating pain. Marc survived the attack.

As recently as May 2006, Marc escorted the U.S. Ambassador from Mexico City to the border between Texas and Mexico. The illegal immigration issue was reaching a boiling point, and the ambassador was getting a firsthand look at the situation. Marc was his bodyguard.

I often wondered if any of the people that called Marc the *?#!*ing Mexican accomplished as much as he did. Twice, I introduced Marc to the crowds where I told his story as part of

The Unstoppable You presentation. Both times he received raucous standing ovations!

Thank God there's life after high school! That's the lesson behind **the little red wheelbarrow...**

It's not where you're at, it's where you're going that makes *The Unstoppable You.*

Lesson 41
The Little
Red Wheelbarrow

AS A TEACHER, I always loved the first day of school! It was time to pry open a few minds. I used the little red wheelbarrow as my crowbar. As the students entered my class, I would greet and hand them a 3x5 card. This card had their seat number on it. They had to look at the seating chart to figure out where to sit. This forced them to think before class even got started.

On the front of the 3x5 card, they had to write their parent's names, address, and phone number. Then I would point to a sketch of my little red wheelbarrow I drew off a design I borrowed from Dr. Denis Waitley. I asked my students to write five comments about the little red wheelbarrow on the back of their 3x5 card. This was my secret test.

The little red wheelbarrow would confuse kids. I had taken something very common — in this case, a wheelbarrow — and redesigned it so it didn't look anything like a normal wheelbarrow. And this was exactly the point of my secret test — to gauge their initial reaction when faced with something new, different, or confusing.

Their responses had nothing to do with the wheelbarrow itself: it was to test their attitudes — positive or negative. Overwhelmingly, in the twenty-plus years that I gave this secret test, the comments were always negative. They ranged from, "It's weird, won't work, that's stupid," to personal attacks on the designer — me!

I often chuckled out loud, reading their comments as I collected them. After I gathered their cards, I'd put them away. Then I would immediately tell them the stories Look for the Pony and When it's Darkest, That's When the Stars Come Out. Class time would end, and I never mentioned the cards again, until the next day.

At the start of the second day, I'd pull out the cards. I would inform them of my secret test. I'd read their comments out loud. The whole class would laugh at some of them.

Eventually some kid would ask, "What's the point?"

That's when I'd tell them, "The point is that you were faced with something new, different, and a little confusing. All I asked you for was five comments, and ninety percent of them were negative. I got very few comments like, 'That's interesting, how does it work, I need more information.'" Then I tell them a real-life story about the little red wheelbarrow...

"How many of you have been to the wave pool in our town?" I asked the class.

Almost every kid raised their hand.

"How many of you had fun at the wave pool and are glad to have one in our little town?"

Once again all hands went up. I then proceeded to tell them how the wave pool almost got washed away, because the city council saw the project as a little red wheelbarrow. The year was 1985. The construction of the local power plant had been completed, and all of the workers left town. Many homes were listed for sale. Most didn't sell; the banks foreclosed. The town, it seemed, was going belly-up. In the midst of those dire times, a tidal wave of controversy stormed over the wave pool project. Most of the town was against the idea. One local doughnut shop had a sign out front that read, "Will the last person to leave Craig please turn off the wave pool?" If I remember correctly, I believe it was going to cost $90,000 to build it. By a narrow three to four margin, the city council voted surf's up; the project was a go.

The first summer the wave pool was completed, I had to test the waters! Even though we're a thousand miles from the nearest ocean, it was hang ten, as the local surfers say! Eventually, the roar of the waves was drowned out by the roar of my stomach. I was hungry and the tide was out. There was no food anywhere. If *I* was hungry, I could only imagine how hungry all the other little "sea urchins" were.

Since there was no concession stand at the wave pool, I later called the city to inquire about putting one in. I asked how many people rode the waves that first summer. I was going to take that number and multiply it by $3 to $5 to figure out how much could be made running a concession stand.

Our town's population at that time had drifted out to sea, and we only had 5,000 people left on board. The rest had abandoned ship! So, I was shocked to hear the pool had 40,000 paid visitations that first summer! That's a lot of hot dogs! Plus, at $2 a head for admission, the pool practically paid for itself. The city informed me that they were going to put in a concession stand, so my plans were shipwrecked. Oh, well...

The point is that the wave pool was viewed with a closed mind by many people in our little town, the same way most of my students perceived the little red wheelbarrow. The pool not only paid for itself that first year, but the city has been splashing in a tidal wave of money ever since.

"Not to mention, how many of you work there?" I asked my kids.

A flood of hands went up!

I challenged my students to always keep an open mind. I told them not to judge people like they did the little red wheelbarrow. Later, I told them about Matt Piotrowski. Many kids perceived Matt as the big red wheelbarrow. With his big red head of hair and his height, he stuck out like a sore thumb. Unfortunately for Matt, much of his time at our high school could be best described as **hammer time...**

The Unstoppable You doesn't judge a wheelbarrow by its color.

Lesson 42

Hammer Time

I HELD THE WOODEN MALLET HIGH over my head. "This mallet is a symbol of today's Friday Story," I said to my class. "It was made by Matt Piotrowski and it's symbolic of the way he was hammered by his classmates."

Matt was a tall, overweight, redheaded kid with a West Virginia accent. Almost immediately, many of his classmates started hammering away at Matt. He was the new kid in town and didn't take to the constant hammering very well.

One day, Matt came to class and threw down his brand-new Sony Walkman, shattering it to pieces. Another day, he punched the cinder block wall and severely hurt his hand. On more than one occasion, I talked to Matt about controlling his temper.

"Don't let those idiots get to you," I told him.

I liked Matt. I felt kinda sorry for him, actually. Most kids don't take the time to really get to know the new kid in town.

Matt really liked my class, and he loved the Friday Stories, so in December of 1998, his mother called and said she needed to talk to me, "It's urgent," she said.

It was Matt's freshman year, and his mom had a strange request. "Would you tell Matt he has to move back to West Virginia with us?"

In all of my years of teaching, I never had a request like that.

My response was, "You're his mother, just tell him he's going."

She told me, "You don't understand. Matt won't leave because of you and your class, especially because of those stories you tell. My husband and I told him he'd have to go, but he refused. If he doesn't go, I'll have to stay here, too!"

I assured her that I would talk to Matt. However, I made her no guarantees that he'd listen. Sure enough, Matt refused to move. He said my class was his favorite ever. His mom stayed behind with him; the rest of his family moved back to West Virginia.

At the beginning of that summer, Matt and his mom packed up their stuff to move back with the family. It seemed like Matt's goodbye lasted all week long. He was over at my house almost every night, along with presents each time! I started wondering if they were ever going to leave. When I waved the final goodbye, I felt a sense of relief — one less kid to raise. I was wrong!

Matt's mother later told me that he recited Friday Story after Friday Story to her nonstop during the four-hour drive to Denver.

Less than a year went by, and in the spring of 2001, I looked up at the door during my last hour class. There stood Matt's mother! She was frantic and needed to talk.

"Matt's threatened to walk back to Colorado. I need to get him back in this class!"

I couldn't believe it! "Here we go again," I thought. I found out after Matt got back to Craig that the kids in West Virginia accused him of being involved in the Columbine High School tragedy. Our high school is over 250 miles away from Columbine! But that didn't matter to the kids in West Virginia. Matt had moved from Colorado, and they wanted to believe it. He was receiving death threats and was asked to leave his school. It was unsafe for him to be there — more hammering...

Matt graduated from our high school in 2003. During his senior year, he was in my class four times a day. That's right — four times a day! He participated in Santa's Wood Shop and made a wooden toy for one of the kids in our town.

Traditionally, on the day of Santa's Wood Shop, all of the kids who made the toys dress up as elves. We call it "Hug an Elf Day."

The kids get recognized for their hard work and get hugged by all of the girls in school. It's a fun day, and the whole school gets into it.

Matt got hugged that day by the hottest girl, one of the varsity cheerleaders. She was also one of the most popular girls, as well. After she hugged Matt, she turned to a friend and said, "That Matt Piotrowski is a ?*#!*ing freak!" She said it loud enough for Matt to hear. The hammering continued...

Matt enlisted in the Navy after high school. Today, he is an aviation mechanic and a Third Class Petty Officer. He called me one night from Japan, and he talked for over an hour and a half. It was great to hear from him and I was glad he didn't call collect! In addition to Japan, Matt had been to Australia, Hong Kong, Guam, South Korea, Singapore, and Thailand. On September 19, 2005, I received a letter in the mail from Commander J.F. Meier of the U.S. Navy. Here's what it said...

---

19 September 2005

Dear Mr. Craig Conrad,
I would like to thank you for the exceptional service Matthew Piotrowski has provided to VAQ-136, the U.S. Navy and this great nation.

Our squadron has been stationed in Japan for over 20 consecutive years, and despite the great distance from home, we have developed into the finest squadron in the Navy. We were recently awarded the Commander Naval Air Forces Pacific Fleet Battle "E" in recognition as the finest EA-6B squadron in the Pacific Fleet. I realize that this accomplishment comes as a result of the hard work and commitment to excellence that the men and women of VAQ-136 exhibit on a day in, day out basis. As part of the Forward Deployed Naval Forces we are called upon to support missions in the Far East and the Southern Pacific Ocean. The "GAUNTLETS" have met these missions with unprecedented success. The squadron has flown nearly every day and we have met every operational commitment in support of our national interests. I could not be more proud of the accomplishments of Matthew and this squadron.

I know full well that this success as a command rides on the shoulders of dedicated professionals like Matthew. The peace and freedom all Americans enjoy is directly attributable to the efforts and commitment of the Sailors of the United States Navy and AMAN Piotrowski is one of the finest I have ever known. I am truly blessed as a Commanding Officer to have such fine men and women make up this great squadron. You can be proud of Matthew, I know that I am!

Again, thank you for your tremendous support. Fly Navy!

> Sincerely,
> J.F. Meier
> Commander, U.S. Navy
> Commanding Officer

A few years ago, I made a scrapbook for the wood shop. It's huge! The pages are about two foot by three foot and you need two hands just to turn them. There's twenty-six years of memorabilia in it. One page has a picture of Matt and the letter from the commander of the U.S. Navy.

On Monday, January 16, 2006, I heard from one of the teachers at school, "Matt Piotrowski is looking for you."

I said, "Impossible! He just called me the night before from West Virginia." He was back home for a few days on leave.

Sure enough, when I got to class, there he was. He and his dad had driven all night to get there. Matt had lost over 100 pounds. He looked the best I had ever seen him! He had came back to say "Hi" and to thank me for the Friday Stories. He also took pictures of his page in the scrapbook.

A few days after Matt left, I went to our local bank. The girl in front of me was the one that called Matt the ?*#!*ing freak.

I asked her, "How are you doing?"

She said she was driving eighty miles a day to work in a restaurant for minimum wage. She asked, "How are you?"

I couldn't resist. I said, "Great. I just saw Matt Piotrowski the other day. He's an aviation mechanic in the Navy. I got a letter from the commander of the U.S. Navy saying what a great job he's doing. Matt's been to Australia, Hong Kong, Guam, Japan, South Korea, Singapore, and Thailand."

She said, "That's nice."

I thought to myself, "You're right. That *is* nice." I reflected on the irony of it all — Matt traveling the world and representing our country, and her working in a restaurant for minimum wage. Sometimes, when you hammer and bend and twist certain types of metal, you help to shape it and make it stronger!

Great job, Matt!!! Don't forget to **dig your pond...**

When life hammers away at you, realize that it's just helping to forge *The Unstoppable You.*

Lesson 43

Dig Your Pond

WHEN I WAS A LITTLE KID, my father took me to this field. Many times we went there and every time it was the same. I ran around and played in the field while my father stood there. It was as if he was imagining something that wasn't there. One day huge "Tonka toys" came to the field. They started to dig a hole much deeper and bigger than anything I could dig with my little Tonka toys. I watched my Dad go down into that hole. He started stacking what looked like big heavy Lego blocks on top of each other. These are some of my earliest memories of watching my dad build our home.

When I got to seventh grade, my father sold that house and bought a farm. We were moving. I didn't want to. I liked the house that Dad built and I didn't want to leave it until I was told the farm had a creek running through it. There was also a fresh water spring.

"The spring," Dad told me, "could be developed into a pond."

When I heard that, I couldn't wait to move. To have a pond of my own — that was a dream come true.

A couple of weeks after we moved to the farm, I went to talk to Dad.

"O.K., let's call the bulldozer guy and start digging the pond," I pleaded.

Dad said, "There's not going to be a bulldozer guy coming."

"O.K. let's call the backhoe guy," I begged.

"Nope, no backhoe guy either," he said.

I was getting mad. I was told I could have a pond. How was I going to have a pond if someone wasn't going to dig it?

"There's a pick, shovel, and a wheelbarrow in the shed," Dad said. "Consider yourself lucky; a lot of kids don't even have that."

That was vintage Dad. If you want it, get it yourself. It's how he was brought up, and he was trying to pass it on. I didn't see it that way. I was a teenager: I felt betrayed.

I told Dad, "Thanks a lot — thanks for nothing."

Years later, that would be the title of a poem I wrote for him. I sent it to him for Father's Day.

Thanks for Nothing

Thanks when I was a baby in the cradle,
for not feeding me with a silver ladle.
Thanks when I was a little boy,
for not buying me every new toy.
Thanks when I was a small tyke,
for not buying me that brand new bike.
And thanks when I became of age and
wanted to go afar,
for not buying me that brand new car.
And later when I went off to college,...
for making me work to acquire the knowledge.
And thanks when I finally got out,
for teaching me what it's all about.
Oh, and thanks for not giving me the money,
when I bought the first house for me and my honey.
Thanks for not giving me all those things I
thought I wanted...for,
really, you gave me so much more.

— Craig Conrad

After I got done feeling sorry for myself, I went to the shed and got the pick, shovel, and wheelbarrow. With an attitude of, "Well, I'll show him," I started to dig. I quickly learned it doesn't take a rocket scientist to operate a shovel: it just takes a willingness to dig. I started digging when I was in seventh grade, and even as a seventh grader, I was smart enough to understand that if I dug one side of the pond and piled the dirt on the other side, I could get twice the pond for half the digging.

Sometimes I'd hit a rock, and then the shovel wouldn't work. That's when I'd use a pick, another piece of highly technological equipment. I kept on digging...

In the eighth grade, the mosquitos and black flies were so bad that I wanted to quit. However, I wanted a pond, so I kept digging. Some days my wheelbarrow would slip off my homemade bridge or tip over. All of the dirt would fall back into the hole I had just dug. I wanted to quit, but I wanted a pond more — so I kept digging...

In ninth grade, I dug into some trees. I needed to use an ax to chop the roots. I'd hook the tractor up with a chain to pull out the stump. The wheels would spin; the stump wouldn't budge. I felt like quitting, but I wanted a pond. *More* digging...

Finally, after three years of digging, one day I dug a shovelful and turned around. It was finished! I did it! Dad helped me put the dam breast in, and my pond was filling up with water. What a day, at long last! My excitement was off the charts when water started to slowly trickle over the spillway. Faster, faster — now the water was gushing over. My dream had become my reality, and I was on cloud nine.

The next day we went to the Lobachsville Trout Hatchery to stock my pond. Dad bought a hundred trout. I could lay in my bed and look out my bedroom window and see my trout rising. I named some of them: Timmy Trout, Randy Rainbow, Betty Brook. It was so cool! I was in heaven for six months. Then hell came!

Hell came in the form of Hurricane Agnus. Pennsylvania didn't get any wind, just seven days of constant rain. Rivers rose twenty-three feet! The Reading area was flooded, as was much of Berks County. The small, gently flowing creek that ran next to my pond had become a violent, raging torrent of water. It totally engulfed my pond, washed out my fish, and destroyed the dam breast. As if that wasn't bad enough, the run off from the neighbor's corn field filled my pond with muck. My pond and Randy Rainbow, Timmy Trout, and Betty Brook were gone. I cried. Three years of digging disappeared in seven days. I cried harder.

My dad walked over to me that day. He saw I was in tears, everything destroyed. He patted me on the shoulder and said, "Sorry, Craig, but you can do it again."

You don't want to hear that when you're a kid. I wanted to hear about the bulldozer coming! But nothing was ever said about the bulldozer coming that day. When I got through feeling sorry for myself the second time, I started digging again. This time I borrowed a page out of my grandfather's story, Rough, Tough and Hard to Bluff. I vowed to build something that would never wash away.

I dug the stones out of the fields like Grandpop did for his house. I dug the sand out of the creek. Dad purchased the cement. There was just one problem: I didn't know a thing about masonry. But I knew someone who did — my grandfather. Together, we built stone raceways that I could raise trout in. It was the last job he did before he passed away.

Almost ten years later — while my son, Colton, was still in diapers — we went back to Pennsylvania to visit my folks. Dad cleaned out the stone raceways and bought some trout. He landscaped and mowed the area around my pond. It looked great! With a rod in one hand and a bottle in the other, Colton caught his first fish in my pond that day. I filmed the whole thing, and that film's worth a million bucks to me. It captures four generations of Conrads whose lives were affected by that pond, from my grandfather who helped me build it, to my son who caught his first fish there.

In the Summer of 2006, I went back to Pennsylvania again. Dad had been diagnosed with cancer, and I was taking him to chemotherapy treatments in Philadelphia. One night, I stopped by the old farm where I grew up. My parents had sold it several years ago. When I told the new owners I was the one who built the stone pond, they said, "We're planning to put trout in there." The stone raceways were still standing.

I never realized as a teenager building my pond that it would actually build me! Thanks Dad for not getting the bulldozer. It taught me *the ripple effect...*

All of you will "dig a pond" someday. That may come in the form of a college education, a new job, or your own business. Just keep digging! The day will come when you scoop your last shovel full and your pond will be finished. That's *Unstoppable!*

Lesson 44

The Ripple Effect

THE PRINCIPAL'S VOICE ON THE INTERCOM shattered my third hour class: "Mr. Conrad, is Aaron Kawcak there?"

"Yes," I responded.

"Please send him to the office immediately," the intercom blared.

All of the kids responded with, "You're in trouble."

Knowing getting pulled from class to go to the office usually isn't a good thing, I asked Aaron what he did. Initially, he said he was going to deny doing anything. However, after he told me what he did and how dangerous it was, I told him to just tell the truth. After all, he told me in front of the whole class! The school's surveillance cameras captured Aaron's "leap of faith" on film. I told him to just be a man and accept responsibility for his actions. As Aaron got up to leave, I mentioned he was lucky to still be alive and assured him that — compared to what could have happened — the punishment he would receive from the office would be nothing.

Aaron's "leap of faith" involved a dangerous and daring jump. Aaron would fly. His flight began on the third floor stair and ended on the second floor commons area — a distance of fifteen to twenty feet. Many kids witnessed his aerial heroics. A couple of feet shorter, and Aaron would have tragically crashed to the first floor below. Still, he and many of the kids in his class questioned why he was being punished. I knew I had to bring my pebble to school on Friday.

Even though I used this lesson and story in the past, I knew I needed to repeat it to Aaron and his class. That Friday, I asked him and his class if they'd ever thrown one of these into a lake. I was holding a small pebble in my right hand. Obviously they all had.

"What happened when you threw it in?" I acted like I didn't know.

"It makes a splash," they said.

"What can you say about the size of the rock and the size of the splash?" was my next question.

Again the class responded with, "The bigger the rock, the bigger the splash."

"Correct!" I yelled while pointing the pebble at Aaron.

"You see, Aaron, your leap of faith was like a big pebble: it created a huge splash."

Aaron and the rest of the class nodded their heads. His leap of faith was the talk of the school for days. Everyone knew about it.

"In part, that's why you were punished," I said. "However, the bigger reason you were punished is because of what happens *after* the splash."

While holding the pebble with my index finger and thumb, I asked the class, "What happens next after the splash?"

"Ripples," they chanted.

"Once again, my young friends, you are correct. Any of you know how far across the lake those ripples go?" I asked.

I faintly heard Aaron reply, "All the way."

While lecturing to the class, but mostly for Aaron's benefit, I explained displacement and how those concentric rings go clear across the lake. This happens even though the ripples are sometimes so small that you can't detect them. The ripple effect goes on and on. It's the same reason why you can be standing on shore and get hit with the wake from a boat five minutes after it's passed by. I gave them more proof, talking about the tsunami that devastated Thailand in 2005. It wasn't the splash that caused the damage; it was the ripple effect.

"Your actions of today are like the splash. However, the ripple effect can go on and on for many years later. That's the reason you were punished, Mr. Kawcak. Imagine if every kid in the school tried that. Would they all make it, Aaron?"

Aaron shook his head no.

"Heaven help the next kid who tries it, 'cause you know one will," I whispered to the class.

Aaron nodded his head in agreement. He and the rest of his classmates understood the meaning of the Friday Story and the ripple effect.

Perhaps Aaron's attitude is typical of most teenagers, because he drew a huge laugh from his class when he said, "I'm still glad I did it!"

I chuckled back and said, "I'm still glad you made it!"

Only time will tell the results of Aaron's leap of faith and its corresponding ripple effect.

I challenged Aaron and his class to make big *positive* splashes. That way, the ripple effect can bring good things to you years later. Such was the case with my fifteen-year-old son, Colton, when he was faced with one of the toughest decisions of his young life — ***the job or the money...***

Your actions of today will ripple out for years
to come, creating *The Unstoppable You!*

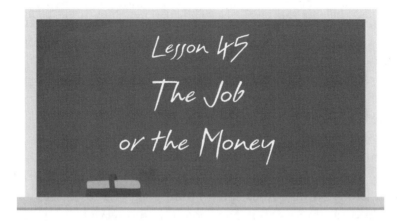

Lesson 45
The Job
or the Money

IN JUNE OF 2005 I RECEIVED A PHONE CALL from Justin Flaherty of Three Forks Ranch. Amazingly, little did I realize at the time that one brief phone call would take my life in a whole new direction. It would also drastically alter my son's adolescence and help forge him into becoming a man. Hopefully, the splash of that initial phone call and its ripple effect will continue to bless the two of us for years to come — proof positive that sometimes it pays to answer your phone!

At that time, Justin was guest activities director at Three Forks Ranch. Reared in Mississippi, his warm southern hospitality made you feel right at home, especially after the first, "Hi, y'all."

Justin was in a bind. He needed a fly-fishing guide to assist with a large group that was coming in that next week. He got a tip from one of their instructors that I had guided for several summers at a private ranch in Meeker, Colorado. When the call came in, I was in the middle of designing a garage and addition I wanted to build on to our house. Guiding fly-fishing was the last thing on my mind.

Initially, I told Justin no thanks. He asked me to reconsider and think about it. I asked him when he needed an answer, and he told me by noon that day! I assured him that I would let him know before noon. As I hung up the phone, I was trying to think of a polite way to tell Justin no thanks again. Luckily, that's when fate and my wife, Vicki, intervened.

Vicki suggested that I mention our son, Colton, as a possibility to help guide. Hearing fishing stories and guiding experiences from Dad at an early age was the culprit. Colton thought he might enjoy guiding. I called Justin right back with an offer he couldn't refuse.

"Justin," I said, "I'll make you a two-for-one deal. I'll bring my fifteen year old son, Colton, along as an apprentice. You can have two guides for the price of one."

Justin said he would have to clear that offer with Jay Linderman, the general manager of the entire Three Forks operation. The last thing Jay needed was another headache. A fifteen year old with no professional guiding experience — now *that* could be a *problem*. But once again, fate intervened. Jay said it was O.K.

During our five days of guiding, I gradually let Colton work with the guests. He took to it well, like a fish to water. He was able to carry on conversations with the adults. Frequently, he'd make them laugh and — just as importantly — they'd catch some fish... some big ones! Several of his guests made the Three Forks Ranch twenty-five-inch club. These are trout that measure twenty-five inches or longer. The guest receives a plaque, and their name is added to the list of other fishermen who caught twenty-five inchers. This list, which includes the guide's name, is proudly displayed in the Three Forks's River Rock Lodge.

River Rock Lodge sits in the middle of 200,000 pristine deeded acres and another 50,000 BLM acres. The Three Forks of the Little Snake River converge on the property, hence the name Three Forks. This is the site of the most extensive and expensive stream restoration in the United States. Millions of dollars was spent to improve over sixteen miles of river.

At the end of our five-day stint, Colton and I returned home. I told him not many fifteen year olds get to go to a place like that, much less work there. I was getting ready to scrapbook that memory in my mind as one great father-son experience when the phone rang. It was Justin calling again.

"Craig, would you and Colton like to guide Bobby Knight, the basketball coach?"

We couldn't pass it up. Back to Three Forks we went. Unfortunately — or fortunately, depending upon how you look at it — Coach didn't show up. Once again, fate intervened...

Because Coach Knight wasn't there, we got to guide Jay Linderman's relatives. Colton and I split them into two different groups: he took one group, and I took the other. They all caught their first trout ever on a fly rod! They went back and told Jay all about it. That did it! We were in! Justin asked if we could stay for nine more days. We stayed!

Before our nine days were over, Justin called me into his office. He wanted to speak to me about Colton. My initial reaction had me wondering, "Uh, oh, what did Colton do?"

I couldn't believe it when Justin asked me if he could hire Colton for the rest of the summer. Wow! What happened during that season would test the metal of any fifteen year old...

Colton was working with Larry Henderson, one of the senior guides. Larry and his wife, Jane, operated the Hidden Valley House. Jane cooked five-star meals, and Larry was an excellent guide with a lifetime of experience. Colton and Larry guided Roger, a very wealthy man, and his wife, Ann. Colton helped Ann catch a twenty-five incher. She received a plaque and her name was added to the list. Roger was so pleased that he left a $6,000 tip. That's right, $6,000!

The tip policy at Three Forks requires that all tips go into a pool, then they're split among all of the guides who worked that week. So all of the guides were going to benefit from this — but Roger wasn't done. He then wrote a check for $600 to Colton as a separate tip. Colton was the only one who could cash it!

When Colton initially received his bonus tip, he was really excited — and he was also confused. He wasn't sure what to do. Knowing the tip policy at Three Forks, he thought he should turn it in. However, Roger was adamant that Colton be the sole recipient.

Colton asked me, "Dad, what should I do?"

Interestingly enough, nearly one hundred percent of those I tell this story to say they would keep the money. And of course, all of my students said the same thing: "Keep the money." Well, I knew that was the wrong answer.

Knowing my advice would be hard to swallow I sat Colton down. "Son," I began, "try to remember this advice the rest of your life. The job is more important than the money." I went on to explain that if he continued to work at Three Forks, he would make a lot more than the $600 tip. Turning it in would be the right thing to do. "Give it to Jay and Justin, and let them decide how to handle it," I said.

The next day, Colton walked into the office at Three Forks and handed his check over to the boss. Now, the total amount of Roger's tips was $6,600. Each guide's take was over $600. Jay and Justin let Colton keep his check and made up the difference with yet another check! Not only that, they hired him for thirty more guide days. The next year, Colton was hired for sixty guide days.

Let's do the math here. That's ninety guide days at $200 a day plus tips (tips average $100 a day). That's approximately $300 a day, or $27,000 total. Which would you rather have — $600 or $27,000? The job really is more important than the money, and honesty is the best policy.

Jay Linderman told me one year later, "If Colton would have kept the check, he would have been done here."

Colton not only secured his job, best of all he also kept his reputation in tact. Exactly the same lesson I wanted the kids to understand the day they tried to ***zap the CSAP...!***

Honesty is the only policy for *The Unstoppable You!*

Lesson 46

Zap the CSAP

IN AN ATTEMPT TO IMPROVE STUDENT APATHY toward taking the state-mandated CSAP test, a fellow teacher, Lance Scranton, and I decided to do something to help improve our test scores. We made a movie called *Zap the CSAP*, which featured a "Rocky-style" fight between me, aka Father Woods, and Lance, aka Brother English. The point of the movie was to illustrate that elective classes like Woods, Band, Art, etc., were just as important as the academics — English, Math, and Science.

The movie was hilarious and very well received at the all-school assembly. It forced kids to think about what their future may hold and to do their best in all their classes, including taking the CSAP. The assembly ended with a raucous standing ovation.

Kids and teachers were going around the school saying, "Zap the CSAP." The State Department of Education got hold of the video and shared it with other schools statewide. It was awesome!

On test day, Lance and I volunteered to take all the discipline-problem kids ourselves, or any kids that were causing any problems during the test. What neither of us ever expected was how many students would be sent to us before the test ever began. As the kids sauntered into our classroom, they thought it was cool that they weren't testing with the rest of their advisory classes: instead, they were testing with the two "movie stars." However, they began wondering why they were there after glancing around the room and seeing their "test mates," none of whom were honor students.

"I'm sure many of you are wondering why you are here today," I began. "The answer should disturb you. This classroom has been called many things, but know this, my young friends, this is where you get sent if you're causing problems or not taking the CSAP test seriously. The reason it should disturb you is because you were sent here before the test even got started. Someone figured you would cause problems, and that judgment was based solely on your reputation. So you see, your reputation got you sent here before your actions had the chance. Much like your shadow, your reputation follows you wherever you go. You are the only one who makes your reputation and are the only one who can break it. So ask yourself this question: What is your reputation saying about you? Unfortunately for many of you, your reputation has preceded you. In other words, your reputation got you here before you did."

After giving the "chosen ones" time to digest these words, I went on to say, "Now, I believe each one of you is not only capable of taking this test, but will do so, answering each and every question. Since this is your last chance if you give us any problems, you'll take your test in solitary confinement in the 'box.'" At that point, I showed them the tiny 4x4 foot sink room where they would be moved to.

"Mr. Scranton and myself will be checking to make sure you take the test correctly and answer all of the questions."

With all eyes focused intently, I asked, "Are there any more questions?"

All heads were shaking no in unison.

"Well, let's begin, and good luck. Oh, and one other thing, if you ever get sent back to this room in the future, you will automatically go to the box."

I'm proud to say Lance and I only sent one kid to the box, and one hundred percent of the test questions were answered. We never had any of the same kids return in the future. Not only did our CSAP scores go up that year, but I'm sure the reputation of some of those students did as well. Because with a good reputation, you can answer yes when asked, *"are you a man of your word...?"*

A good reputation is the foundation for
The Unstoppable You.

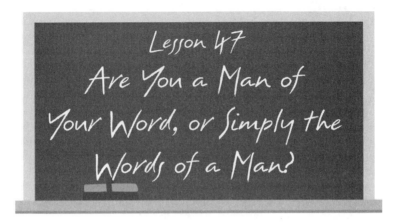

ONE FRIDAY, I ASKED MY CLASS a simple question: "What's the most valuable thing in your possession?"

Their responses were humorous to downright hilarious. Answers ranged from cell phones and wallets filled with cash to their girlfriends.

When I stopped laughing, I redefined the question. "I'm looking for something internal, not external."

After hearing answers like, "My heart, my brain, my eyes," I would nod in agreement.

"While those things are obviously vital to your existence, the thing I'm looking for is something you're not born with," I said. "You acquire it. No one can give it to you, and you are the only one who can give it away. Most importantly, it defines who you are."

I pointed to a picture of a very large diamond I drew on the chalkboard. "It's your precious gem," I told the puzzled class.

Now that they were totally confused, and I had their undivided attention, I gave them the answer.

"It's your word and the way you honor your commitments."

As I continued on, I explained to the class that a person's word is like a precious gem. Its value is priceless because it determines who you are. When you give your word to someone, you just gave away that precious gem. The cool part is when you keep your word and honor your commitments, you get your precious gem back. A high level of trust is formed between you and the person or persons you gave your word to, because something of great value was exchanged. The bad news is when you break your word and your commitments, you don't get your precious gem back, or the level of trust. Frequently, both are lost forever.

"How many of you have had a friend break their word or commitment with you?" I asked.

Every single kid raised their hand.

"And the precious gem?" I asked while raising both arms high in the air.

"Lost!" the class shouted in unison.

My lesson that Friday was to keep your word and honor your commitments, no matter what the cost. Be careful who you give that precious gem to, because you must get it back! Otherwise, you lose the trust and quite possibly the relationship as well. To help drive that lesson home, I told them the emotional story of **George and Dave...**

Keep your word, honor your commitments,
and create the precious gem that is
The Unstoppable You!

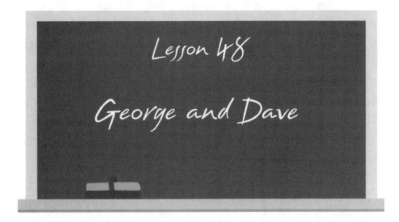

Lesson 48

George and Dave

GEORGE AND DAVE MET IN THE SEVENTH GRADE. Each of them had gone to different elementary schools. However, both boys were the same. They had similar interests, similar abilities, and similar likes and dislikes. They even looked so much alike that they could have been brothers. Classmates sometimes even got them confused.

When George and Dave were the first two chosen for their seventh grade basketball team, they developed a friendship that lasted throughout high school. People say if you graduate from high school with one true friend, you're lucky...because that one true friend will be there for you no matter what, through thick and thin — forever. George and Dave believed that to be true. Both of them knew that the other was that one true friend, and they were good with that.

Dave got a car his junior year and almost every night, he gave George a ride home after basketball practice. Dave drove miles out of his way to take George home. They both had fun on those rides home, because Dave had an eight-track tape player and good speakers in his car. George, ever so grateful, promised to someday give Dave a ride. A lot of them, too!

After high school, George went to college, and Dave went to work. Although they didn't see each other as much, their friendship never diminished. When they got together, they would frequently reminisce about that championship basketball game against their archrival, Mt. Penn.

Dave fell down in the three-second lane with the ball. With no one to pass to and the referee about to blow the whistle, he threw the ball toward the basket. Swish! They went on to win the game by two points! George would laugh remembering that shot and tell Dave he was a better shot shooting from his knees. Dave would laugh, too, and nod his head in agreement.

After George graduated from college, he started his own business. Dave was still working at the same place since high school. One day, George's mom, Delores, showed up at her son's work place. She was crying and said she had some bad news. It was one of those moments George would never forget, just like he would forever remember where he was and what he was doing when President Kennedy was shot, or when the New York Twin Towers came down during the 9/11 tragedy. George's mom told him that Dave was in a coma in critical condition. He was in a hospital in New Jersey. George immediately called the hospital.

The phone rang several times and then a sobbing voice answered, "Hello."

It was Dave's mother. She told George that Dave was diving into the ocean when he broke his neck. Some guy saw him floating out in the water, and he swam out and pulled him to shore. Dave was unconscious. No one knew how long he'd been out there. Dave's mother told George that the doctors said if Dave lived, he would be paralyzed for life. She held the phone up to Dave's ear. She said maybe the sound of George's voice would pull him out of the coma. It was the first time George had ever talked to Dave without laughing.

His voice cracking with emotion, George talked about all of the good times the two had shared growing up. Tears streamed down his cheeks as he reminded Dave he had fallen down before and made a good shot. George encouraged his buddy to take another shot now. He also remembered his promise to give Dave a ride if he ever needed one.

He told his best friend that if he took another shot and made it, George would give him as many rides as he needed. If Dave needed a lift, George would lift him. George vowed to become Dave's legs, because George truly believed that had the situation been reversed, Dave would have done the same for him.

Unfortunately, Dave never got to see how committed George was: he died shortly after the phone call. George kept his word anyway. Within the next year, George married and moved thousands of miles away. As a tribute to his best friend, George walked or rode his bike to work every single day for twenty-six years — even on the coldest day, when the temperature was 61 degrees below zero, or when snow was about two-and-a-half feet deep.

George never drove a vehicle to work in twenty-six years, no matter what the weather conditions, all because of a promise he'd made and the belief that your word is like a precious gem. George believed that someday he'd get it back when he and Dave met again in heaven.

I know this story is true, because even though most people know me as Craig, few people realize my first name is George. Dave was my best friend and teammate.

I still think about Dave after all these years. I'm happy to say I never broke my word to him, and I can live with that. What I couldn't live with was hearing one of my students, Wacie Laabs, breaking his word to his friend and teammate, Billy Ivy. It was in the Fall of 2004, and it happened right in front of me in my classroom. I knew the story I'd tell that Friday would be ***five minutes of hell...***

Keeping your word is *Unstoppable!*

Lesson 49

Five Minutes of Hell

WACIE LAABS AND BILLY IVY WERE TEAMMATES on our high school baseball team. They were classmates, too. Both of them were in the same woodworking class I taught.

It was an ordinary day in the Fall of 2004 when the two of them came into class. Wacie asked Billy if he could borrow a dollar to buy a pop from the pop machine. Billy gave Wacie a buck, and Wacie bought a pop. Nothing unusual there. In fact, I've seen kids do that hundreds of times. What would make this seemingly insignificant event turn out to be an unforgettable Friday Story is because of what *did not* happen next.

Wacie promised Billy he'd pay him back the next day, but then he told Billy the following day, "I forgot." He promised to bring him the dollar tomorrow. Once again the next day, Wacie forgot.

Billy then challenged Wacie by asking him, "Are you a man of your word, or simply the words of a man?" A famous quote he learned from his Wood's teacher — me!

The entire class jeered and gestured at Wacie, saying, "Oooh, Oooh!"

Wacie stood up, feeling the pressure from his class. "I swear on the Marine's honor I'll bring your dollar tomorrow!" He bellowed in front of the entire class.

Wacie sat down and the jeering ceased. Everyone, including me, knew how important the Marines were to Wacie.

Wacie wanted to be a Marine ever since he was in fifth grade. He talked about them constantly, and he could tell you facts and strategies of some of their greatest battles. He knew the names of all the soldiers in the famous picture of the American flag raising on Iwo Jima. I felt he knew more about the Marines than the Marines knew about themselves. So the next day, after Wacie "forgot" about Billy's dollar once again, I knew what I had to do. I called in the Marines — literally!

Honor, courage, and commitment are part of the core values of the Marines. Cory Hixson was one of my former students who learned those values becoming a Marine. He lost his eye, and almost his life, in the war in Iraq. He was back in town on leave, so I called him and told him what was going on. I asked him if he would come in and be a "live" Friday Story. Cory agreed, having remembered the effect the Friday Stories had on him when he was in my class.

When word got out 'round school that Cory Hixson, a hometown hero, was going to be the special live Friday Story, more than 200 students and teachers showed up in my classroom. We had to move out into the wood shop just so everyone could squeeze in. Kids were sitting on the floor, the table saws, the work benches, and anywhere they could find a place.

I began by introducing Cory to the crowd while showing a picture of him doing the Five Minutes of Hell. The Five Minutes of Hell is a wall sit usually reserved for those who come late to class. In Cory's case, it was for leaving early one day along with the rest of the class. The picture showed Cory and his brother, Greg, and the entire class "doing the five," as we like to say. The picture was quite funny.

When everyone stopped laughing, I said, "Cory went from Five Minutes of Hell to the real thing."

Lance Corporal Hixson bravely stepped up in front of some of his former classmates in the same exact shop in which he had built a Grandfather clock his senior year. Over 200 kids sat in stone silence, waiting to hear what this hometown hero would say, while trying not to stare at his missing eye or his scarred face.

He began by saying his father was a Marine in Vietnam.

"Ever since I was a little boy, I wanted to be a Marine, too," Cory softly said.

Ironically, after watching him graduate from Marine boot camp in 2003, his brother, Greg (another former student), enlisted on the way home. Within a few short months, they were together in Iraq, carrying on the family tradition and wearing the same uniform that Dad wore in 'Nam.

"Being a grunt and being able to look down upon a dirty, bloody, and sweat-stained uniform was what I wanted out of life," Cory said of his decision to enlist.

He then told the crowd about the five-hour battle in Fallujah. "After the battle, we were checking on enemy pickup trucks we had attacked, when a mortar round exploded next to me." Cory was taken to a hospital in Iraq, where he awoke in a haze of pain, missing one eye.

"Everything's going to be all right," he heard a familiar voice say. Looking up with his one good eye, he saw a fellow Marine — his brother, Greg.

Cory spoke that Friday about the value of honor, courage, and — most of all — commitment.

"The importance of keeping your word, no matter how big or small, is everything in the Marines and in life."

The 200-plus students hung on every word Cory said that day — and there was one, especially, who was taking his message to heart. You guessed it — Wacie Laabs.

When Cory finished, I had Wacie present him with a Brother Woods shirt to show our appreciation. Cory graciously accepted the shirt and thanked everyone. Then he did something I couldn't believe! He removed the Marine emblem from his uniform, turned, and handed it to Wacie.

"Don't ever make me regret giving this to you," Cory said to a misty-eyed Wacie.

The crowd exploded! *I* even got choked up!

Afterward, Wacie thanked me, knowing that that Friday Story was especially for him. He told me that someday he was going to be a Marine.

"When my years of service are over, I'm going to give my Marine emblem to Cory Hixson," he said.

On September 14, 2006, Wacie became a Marine. He currently is Private First Class Laabs, part of MSOB (Marines Special Operations Battalion), and has several more years to go.

I can only hope I get to witness the day when Cory gets his emblem back. I'm almost positive it will be with no regrets! Oh, I forgot to mention — Billy got his dollar back, too!

Thanks, Cory and Wacie, for helping to perpetuate a *Tradition of Excellence...*

The Marine's core values are *Unstoppable*!
What's your code of honor?

Lesson 50

A Tradition of Excellence

DURING MY TWENTY-SIX YEARS OF TEACHING, I was honored by my students six times when they nominated me for Who's Who Best Teachers in America. On March 18, 1993, I was presented with the Governor's Award for Excellence in Education by Colorado Governor Roy Romer.

My classes were featured in seven different national magazines. In the spring of 2001, *Wood*, the world's largest woodworking magazine, ranked our program as one of the Top Shops in the world. In 2002, I was selected to run with the Olympic torch for the Salt Lake City Winter Olympics.

ABC's and NBC's local evening news, and CBS's *The Early Show* featured segments on their news programs about the Friday Stories and our unique classroom innovations. On May 25, 2005, I received a "Tradition of Excellence," a national award presented by the Woodcraft Corporation. This award was initiated nationwide and titled "A Tradition of Excellence" in honor of my classroom. I was the first teacher in the country to receive it. And even though I've been the recipient of these accolades, I give all of the credit to my students: they are the ones who earned it through *their* Tradition of Excellence. Here's a small sample of some of the things they did...

2 X 4M

The 2 X 4M was a contest to find the most creative woodworking student. Contestants had to create and build something using one 2 X 4 stud. Any wood that was wasted counted against that student, and no other materials could be used. Matt Beckett took top honors and won a cash prize his senior year. His creation was a unique television tray he designed. Many years later, Matt would use his creativity as the designer and owner of his own business, The Sign Source. Matt helped me design the Brother Woods logo and the Tradition of Excellence T-shirts I give to deserving students. He earned my trust when he returned a $600 check: the school bookkeeper mistakenly paid him twice for some work he had done for me. Matt could have easily kept the money, as I would never have known. The day he returned it, he lost $600 — but he gained my respect. So, when the Woodcraft Corporation needed 600 Tradition of Excellence T-shirts designed and created, I called Matt. He's earned that $600 many times over since that day.

Boxes to Buildings

Dave Gobbo won the 2 x 4M contest his senior year with his vanity mirror. Dave grew up in Maybell, Colorado — population under 100. It's the home of the annual "Where the hell is Maybell?" bike ride. Dave had to get up at 5:00 each morning to do his chores and get to school — about forty miles away — on time. I was teaching Zero Hour that year. Classes started at 7:00 a.m., one hour before the normal school day began. Dave was never late. Not once! His projects were an unbelievable display of craftsmanship. In the summers, he worked as a laborer for a local contractor. But not anymore! Dave rose from those humble beginnings to become project superintendent for Adolfson and Peterson Construction Company. He went from building $10 boxes in my class to building 34 million dollar buildings. Dave came back to my wood shop in 2004 and did a live Friday Story. He told the kids how he used to be in the same class, sitting in the same seats. He spoke about how the Friday Stories helped forge him, from the little kid from Maybell, into the man he'd become. He thanked me for the Friday Stories in front of all my students.

Dave verified what I tell my kids every year: "The most important project we build isn't even made of wood...it's you!"

Thanks, Dave. That's excellent!

Out of the Bucket

Author's note: Even though I was granted permission to use this student's real name, I chose to change it to protect him and his family. You'll understand why after reading his letter.

The major theme behind Lesson #24 Crabs in the Bucket is to get out of the bucket, before it's too late. Unfortunately for too many kids, they're born into that bucket. Whether the bucket is poverty, drug or alcohol abuse, or crime, their destiny is doomed from the start. Just like the crabs that don't make it out of the bucket, these kids are all too often thrown into a "boiling pot" and are "eaten up."

Fortunately, every once in awhile, one is able to pull himself out of the bucket, breaking free from the other crabs. This is the story about how James got out of the bucket, and it's best told by James himself. I received his letter in 2007:

Sir,

I am sure you probably do not remember me. I was that kind of child. I was easily forgotten or overlooked. However, I was in your Woods Shop class for three years, from 1994-1996. I remember at that time school was not very important to me. I didn't make poor grades; it just was not that important academically. School for me was a release from an alcoholic father and drug-abusing mother. My home life was nothing any child should be part of. School was my sanctuary, and wood shop was some place I could go and make something. My projects were never really any good. I'm no fool: I was lucky if I could successfully put a box together. However, I loved wood shop.

I never attempted the fourth year of woods because, after a failed suicide attempt, I ran away from home. I went to Phoenix and lived on the streets for 13 months. I did things I will never be proud of to survive, and I committed horrible crimes against my fellow man. I was a terrible young man with no urge to change. I was arrested for assault the first time and faced criminal charges of seven days in jail, probation, community service, and restitution for the injured party. The second progressively got more stern with the punishment and then time; number three ended me up in a minimum security prison for six months. Prison is by far the worst thing, I have been homeless, and now have gone to war. Prison is the worst. It makes you strong, it makes you think, it makes you look at life in a way one can only see in prison.

I was released from prison at first to work furlough, then permanently, and still did not change. It wasn't until I had my best friend die in my arms from a shooting that took place over business that should not have been going on did I finally get the message. By this time I was 19. Throughout the entirety of these events I had myself, and that was it. No one was available for guidance, direction, or support. I could only think about lessons learned. Lessons that got me shot, stabbed, and nearly pummeled to death, but worse killed the one person I did have in my life that I could trust. The one thing I could remember from school was not when to put a comma or how to find the area of a right triangle, it was your lesson. The UNSTOPPABLE lessons.

No matter what happened to me, I knew I would make it through. Lessons that you took the time to teach taught me that. I never looked at them in that light when I was 14, 15, and 16. I needed them only three short years later. The story is a success in some portions. I have cleaned up my act. I am in the United States Air Force and serving my country proudly. I have a loving wife, a 4-year-old daughter, and one on the way. I have finished high school. I have two baccalaureate degrees, my masters, and I will finish my Ph.D. in December. I have followed timidly in your giant footsteps and have traveled around speaking to troubled youth about making mistakes and living, learning, and eventually succeeding.

This is in a large part due to you, and I sincerely, from the bottom of my heart, thank you for taking time to deliver a life message to kids that have yet to experience it. My actual life, my success, and happiness are in my control, but the motivation and perseverance came from the beginning stages of THE UNSTOPPABLE YOU.

God Bless sir!
James Moyer, SSgt, USAF
Contract Specialists
82 Contracting Squadron

Congratulations, James, for getting out of the bucket. I'm darn proud of you! Now you can start your own *Tradition of Excellence!*

"Chops"

His name is Garrett Schopper, and I nicknamed him "Chops." He earned his Master Key (self-discipline) when he was a freshman in my class. He shook my hand, making a commitment to be Unstoppable (drug and alcohol free.) Since that time, Chops has visited twenty-two different countries. In many of them, he was of legal drinking age. I am happy to report that Chops has remained Unstoppable!

Chops graduated from the prestigious Johnson and Wales University with cum laude honors in just three-and-a-half years. He earned a scholarship from Syracuse-Sejong University and is currently studying in Seoul, South Korea, as part of his MBA program. By the time he graduates, he will have studied in four countries: Sweden, South Korea, China, and the United States.

Chops earned my respect the day I challenged him and his Zero Hour class to never be late. Zero Hour was a special class time our school offered for students, when they could meet an hour before the normal school day started. The purpose of Zero Hour was to provide kids an opportunity to take a class they couldn't squeeze into their schedule. Several different classes were offered. As you can well imagine, Zero Hour was plagued by tardies and absenteeism. I dared Chops and the Zero Hour class to do something that had never been done before.

"I challenge you to earn a Master Key by disciplining yourself to never be late: you cannot have one tardy for the entire class all year."

The whole class embraced the challenge.

One dark and snowy morning, the roads to school were covered with ice. Chops, not wanting to be late to class, was driving too fast for conditions. His car slid off the road and got stuck in the ditch. Knowing he didn't have much time left to get to class, he hitched a ride with a passerby, only to discover a huge traffic jam snarled on the hill leading to the school. Cars were stuck or sliding everywhere. He knew he'd be late if he waited any longer. At that point, he thanked the passerby for the ride, jumped out of the car, and ran over a half mile through at least twelve inches of snow. Chops got to class ten seconds before the tardy bell rang. That year was the only time in our school's history that no one was ever late to Zero Hour.

Garrett Schopper not only earned his Master Key that day, he continues to use it to open door after door of opportunity. But, I feel sorry for his children when he has a family of his own someday. Just imagine how many times those kids are gonna hear how Dad ran to school through a foot of snow — uphill — no less!

Congratulations, Chops! Keep up the great work and stay Unstoppable! That's excellent!

7 Lakes

As word spread about our shop's Tradition of Excellence, some once-in-a-lifetime opportunities opened up for some of my kids. One of those opportunities came in the form of a phone call from Steve Herter, the manager of the newly constructed 7 Lakes Lodge in Meeker, Colorado. This exclusive lodge catered to the rich and famous. The cost for two people for a five-day visit was about $10,000.

Steve was inquiring to see if I had three students who wanted to build three cedar strip canoes for the lodge. He offered to pay for all of the materials for six canoes.

"That way the kids can each build one for themselves at no cost," Herter said.

Brandon Balleck, his brother, Kyle, and Matt Smith took on the challenge of building the six canoes. One canoe usually takes a whole year for a kid to build, but these guys were going to build two each. They did an exquisite job.

When the canoes were completed, Steve invited the three boys and their families to the lodge for the day. I got to go, too! They treated us like high rollers. We were served gourmet food and had unbelievable accommodations. Excellent fishing — complete with professional guides — rounded out the day. *Nine News* from Denver came and interviewed us while we were there. It was awesome!

As we were leaving, Steve asked me if I would like to guide fly-fishing trips for the guests in August. I wasn't going to let that opportunity slip by.

"Absolutely," I told him.

Among the many rich and famous, I also met the Prime Minister of Israel, the CEOs of IBM, AOL, the president of World Bank, and one of the major civil rights figures in American history. Not too shabby for a high school wood shop teacher. In fact, that's excellent!

The Wood Show

At the end of each school year, I display all of the projects my students create at our annual Tradition of Excellence wood show. Former students come back to judge and award the top prizes. Many of the students who displayed a Tradition of Excellence in high school went on to do so in the real world, as well. There's too many to mention them all.

Roger Corey won Best of Show his senior year. He was the first student to build a pool table, and many followed his lead. Roger built it for his dad. His dad choked back tears when he saw it. Roger eventually took over his dad's business, Corey Electric. I called him to do some electrical work for me one day, and he showed up right away. He worked for several hours, and when he left, he refused to be paid.

Roger said, "I owe you for all those Friday Stories. I think about them everyday."

Brothers

I taught many brothers throughout the years, and few of them were like the Hesses. They were the same brothers who got into trouble with their mom for sanding their woods projects in the living room. They covered everything with sawdust! They said it was worth it, because they both won Best of Show during their senior years.

Eric Hess was a shy, quiet freshman who stuttered, so he didn't talk very much. Ryan Hess, the exact opposite, wouldn't shut up. I introduced them to the weight room when they were freshmen. I really felt it would help their confidence, especially Eric's. To this day, I still tease them about how they were barely able to bench press a hundred pounds. Now after competing in the Natural Strength Association Colorado State Championship in 2003, they tease me. Ryan dead-lifted 680 pounds, and together the brothers "lifted" their team to a second-place finish, with 19 first-place awards and a combined lift of more than 4,000 pounds.

Ryan became our hometown deputy sheriff. Eric graduated from Fort Lewis College in 2006, and as I write this, he is student teaching at our high school. He is applying for a physical education job opening next year because of a retirement.

Eric was a live Friday Story in 2004. It's nice to think he could soon be telling Friday Stories himself in the room next to mine. It's the same room where his Tradition of Excellence began — the weight room.

Running Like the Wind

Kelly Christensen was the youngest of four brothers. I taught all of them for four years each. I literally had at least one Christensen in my class for over twelve years. What a Tradition of Excellence Micah Christensen, the oldest, started! He won Best of Show his senior year, and his brothers — Kris and Andrew — won their senior years, too!

Kelly was no different. He made a solid walnut sleigh bed his senior year, the wood alone costing almost $1,000. Kelly won Best of Show, keeping the Tradition of Excellence alive — not just in my classroom, but in his own living room, as well.

Kelly kept the tradition of excellence in sports, too — but instead of choosing football, as his brothers had, he decided to run cross-country. Since he was favored to win the state championships his senior year, I drove over 500 miles to watch the race. I arrived just as the runners were "taking their mark." Kelly waved and grinned at me right before the gun sounded.

"Go!" I yelled.

Kelly took off running like the wind, taking the lead. Unfortunately the wind would change direction, and Kelly finished fifth. It was a great accomplishment, considering over 200 people ran the race, but a disappointed and teary-eyed Kelly didn't think so.

I told him after the race, "You're still the champ in my book."

Kelly was voted "outstanding senior boy" at graduation. But I knew he wasn't truly satisfied: he had some unfinished business to take care of.

On May 29, 2004, in Pomona, California, he took care of it. Racing against the best runners in the country, including some of those who beat him at the state meet, Kelly won the National Steeple Chase Championship.

He autographed his championship picture and I put it in our Tradition of Excellence scrapbook in my classroom. He wrote, "Part of this title belongs to the Friday Stories." Now Kelly's the champ in *his* book, too! That's excellent!

A Letter From Beth

I received this letter in my school mailbox the first week of May 1997. It was from a former student, Beth McMillan. Beth was so quiet and shy that she hardly ever spoke in my class. I teased and joked with her constantly, just to get her to open up. I could see great potential in her, but she needed to see it in herself.

Beth loved the Friday Stories, and I never realized the impact they had on her until I read her letter...

Mr. Conrad,

As a former student of yours, I want to thank you for what you do as a teacher. I completed Woods I (89-90) and got partially through Woods II (90-91) when my family moved to Quincy, Illinois. I did not want to move, for I was comfortable with the atmosphere of my hometown. Truth was, I was a shy and reserved individual who didn't have a lot of goals for herself. I figured I would go to beauty school (I would have stunk) instead of college, stay in town, and that's "all she wrote."

When we got to Illinois, I remained uninvolved in school and desperately missed home. Far removed from my Colorado friends, I didn't want anything from Quincy High except the diploma that meant I could return to my mountains. I wasn't quite miserable, [being homesick for Colorado] but headed there first.

There were many events that turned my apathy to activity, but as I began to realize that Quincy was a clean opportunity to be whatever the heck I wanted to be, your Friday Story times kept running through my mind. I strove for excellence in everything I did as I finished high school. I graduated in 1993 having been swim team captain, an active member of the Thespian Club, Concert Choir, Show Choir, and Madrigal Choir. It was rare for a "newcomer" to be a part of the Show and Madrigal Choirs because of "politics." You have to "pay your dues" first. But politics are among the obstacles we see when we take our eyes off the goal — that is something I never did.

I will graduate in May with a music degree from the University of Illinois with a very impressive resume, thanks to God's rich blessing and providence. However, the reason I tell you this is that my degree is in Music Education. Because of the impact you had on me as a student, I want to touch lives as you have touched mine. I realized during my student teaching that this is an exhausting job with little thanks. Teachers put so much into each day, and never know if they make a difference because students don't realize so until later in life (if ever!). You invest in your students, Mr. Conrad, and I pray those investments return to you ten-thousand fold.

I have seen the shop featured in a woodworking magazine, and I'm not surprised that the program has grown in such a wonderful way. I am so thankful to have that shop as a part of my background. You taught us so much more than woodworking by taking precious time to contribute to our character. Don't ever stop.

> Thank you, Mr. Conrad.
> Your former student,
> Bethany M. McMillan

I'd like to believe that every Friday somewhere in Illinois, just before the music kids take out their instruments or get ready to sing, their teacher, Beth McMillan, shares a story of hope and inspiration. I'd also like to believe that some little kid in that class is listening to those stories — some little kid who doesn't even realize that someday he or she will become a teacher. A teacher who will share stories of hope and inspiration with their students, all because of the effect Beth McMillan had on them when they were kids. That's Unstoppable! That's a *Tradition of Excellence!*

Kayak to Commander

Khris Johns loved the water ever since he was a little kid. In high school, he loved wood shop. His senior year, he won Best of Show when he combined his two loves and built a kayak. Khris launched his kayak in the high school swimming pool. It was his maiden voyage, but not his last. This was the same pool he swam in while on the swim team. Did I mention Khris loved the water?

Is it any wonder that Khris went to the Coast Guard Academy after high school? After graduating from the Coast Guard he became LTJG Khris Johns, Commanding Officer of the USCGC *Halibut* in Marina Del Ray, California.

Khris returned to the wood shop and was a live Friday Story. He told the kids about harrowing rescues at sea. Stories of thirty foot swells and stormy seas at night had my classes riveted to his every word.

Khris said, "The Friday Stories left me with goose bumps as I considered the goals I had set for my life. It made me set priorities. I was no longer just thinking about what I was going to do for the weekend, but what I was going to do with my life! The Friday Stories taught me not to be afraid to reach for the 'impossible.'"

Khris and I had a great laugh when he finished his live Friday Story. That's when I asked him, "Do you remember the day we conned your mother into buying us lunch?"

Khris's mom was a counselor at our high school. She had just given him over $100 his senior year to buy special marine paint for his kayak.

Khris was really nervous that he might mess up and have to buy more paint, so I helped Khris and he did an excellent job. To show his appreciation, he offered to take me to lunch. I graciously accepted.

That's when he told me, "I don't have any money."

Figuring his mom wouldn't give him anymore after buying the paint, we devised a plan. Khris would tell his mom he spilled the paint, and he needed to buy more. When she'd get her checkbook out, he would tell her he was just kidding, he only needed $15. His mother, sensing relief at not having to buy more paint at $100 a gallon, would easily fork over $15 for lunch.

The plan worked to perfection. I'll never forget the look on his mom's face when Khris told her he had spilled the paint. Nor will I forget how she laughed and yelled at the both of us after we got the lunch money and confessed our con job. That was excellent!

The Warrior

Almost every day I would ask Henry Billett the same question: "What did you do to win the state championship last night?"

Many of Henry's classmates were confused. They knew Henry was a wrestler, but the season didn't start for another three-and-a-half months. So, why was I asking Henry that question? Because Henry was a warrior. Every day, he'd answer that question with something he had done the night before to better his odds at wrestling. The question I'd ask repeatedly was as much for Henry as it was for all of his classmates. It was to show them all that to be a champion, one had to be a warrior each and every day.

Henry was more than just a warrior in spirit; he enjoyed searching for arrowheads and relics from warriors of long ago. Henry had an impressive collection. He designed and constructed a wood and glass display table in the shape of an arrowhead in my Woods class. Henry, the warrior, took Best of Show honors with it.

After bugging him all year with questions, Henry the warrior qualified for the state wrestling championship. He would do battle with his arch nemesis, who Henry had never beaten in all their previous wars. But a true warrior doesn't worry about the past or the battles lost. The warrior had been training every day for this.

I took my wife, Vicki, and my son, Colton, to see the much-anticipated battle. I drove over 500 miles, arriving just in time to see Henry and his arch nemesis walk out onto the mat. What a war it was! With four seconds left in the match, and the score tied 2-2, they went out of bounds. Henry would be on the bottom and his opponent on top when the match resumed. I was screaming to Henry as loud as I could, watching the last four seconds tick off the time clock. As the clock ran out, the warrior did not. Henry scored a two-point reversal! The warrior did it! He was the best 112-pound wrestler in the state!

After graduating from high school, Henry started his own business while at college. The business combined extreme sports promotion with Henry's very own clothing line. The name of his business: Warrior Racing and Warrior Competition Apparel. Were you expecting something different? Once a warrior, always a warrior. That's excellent!

Kippy the Kid

Kip Hafey was in my mass-production class the year they set a record, selling 310 video cases. Kip was also the starting quarterback for our football team. I liked Kip, and he liked me.

One night, he and two of his friends got together to show their appreciation. They decided to toilet paper my yard. Just as the mischievous trio were finishing their "paper work," they spotted headlights coming around the corner. They were sure it was me. They quickly hopped in their car and tore off. The headlights kept getting closer, so they went faster. Still the headlights got closer.

"Go! Go!" Kip kept yelling to his friend driving the get-away car.

So, his friend went even faster. They went through not just one or two, but six stop signs. The headlights kept getting closer. Suddenly, flashing lights appeared.

"Hey, since when does Mr. Conrad drive a police car?" the driver asked Kip.

"He doesn't! It's the cops! Pull over!" Kip yelled.

Oh, what a sight the three of them were, standing at my doorstep with the police officer.

Kip said, "We did it 'cause we like you."

I tried to look mad and told them they would have to rake my entire yard the next day. They agreed. I closed the door and just started laughing. The next day, my yard was cleared of all the leaves and toilet paper.

Kip Hafey is now the science teacher and head football coach at the same high school where I taught him. My son, Colton, had him for outdoor science and football this year. Colton really liked Mr. Hafey.

"So, watch out Mr. Hafey, you know what happens next!" After all, you started *that* tradition.

"Darwood"

Darren Cattoor never won Best of Show honors. He took the class, like many others, because of the Friday Stories. I nicknamed him "Darwood."

The Friday after the Columbine High School tragedy, I challenged all of my students, "What would you do to stop a similar tragedy from happening at our school?"

Over 100 kids heard that challenge, but Darwood was the only one to take the initiative. He asked for permission to read his thought provoking statement over the intercom to the entire school that Friday.

> "I would like to say some things about the recent events that have occurred last week. One reason I have to say something is that a question was posed to me. The question was, If you knew that a person was planning such a horrible event, how would you stop it? And as I thought through answers like call the police, tell a teacher, and talk to a parent, I heard Mr. Conrad say that no matter what we answered, he was

going to keep asking us what we would do to stop this from happening — to see how long we were willing to fight to keep this from happening. This question really made me think about what we can do to stop stuff like this.

"Please answer the following questions in your own mind if you do, or plan to do, any of the following:

1. Do you enjoy having a day off of school to do whatever you choose to do that day?

2. Do you enjoy the company of your friends in and out of school?

3. Do you have goals for the future? Do you have things you want to do in life?

"I hope you all have answered yes, because if you did, we all have some common ground with each other. This means no matter how diverse each of our lives are, we all have some common interests. I also believe that we all have a love for life in common, so WHAT WILL YOU DO TO STOP THIS?

THEN WHAT WILL YOU DO?
Maybe tell a cop, teachers, and parents.
THEN WHAT WILL YOU DO?
Be more open to people's views and
  concerns on life.
THEN WHAT WILL YOU DO?
Maybe try being an example of tolerance.

"We all have common goals and interests. Let's live life and accomplish these goals. Let's try and extend a hand to those who don't have the friends and support that many of us do. Let's better ourselves and others through following the paths in life we want to excel in and be happy in. And, let's make a stand to do the best we can to keep this from happening in our school, our friend's schools, and our relative's schools. You might be the one who makes the difference that saves lives. WHAT WILL YOU DO?"

Darren is married with kids of his own now. He keeps the Tradition of Excellence alive by sharing many of the lessons he learned through the Friday Stories. Hopefully, this is paving the way for a safer environment in the future for his kids. That's excellent!

Unstoppable Shops

The year after I was hired back after being RIFed, I faced a crisis: either turn the Woods program around or have it shut down, just like hundreds of others all over the country. I was given one year to perform this magic.

Instead of pulling a rabbit out of my hat, I hired the kids to do the magic. Each year in my Woods II class we'd pick a project to mass-produce. After making one project for each student in the class, they were given an opportunity to sell as many as they could in five days.

They would take their sample project door to door, earning a paycheck for each order they took, plus a profit for the shop as well. This Unstoppable Shop concept saved my program and hundreds of others around the country. Thanks in part to all of the magazine and media coverage, many other shop teachers started doing the same thing in their own wood shops.

I also held several three-day workshops for teachers from all across the United States. My students brought in tons of money through the years, so we were able to purchase any new tools or machines we wanted. I never had to beg the school district for money, because we were totally self-sufficient. Best of all is what it did for the kids: it helped them to raise the bar so they could be part of the Thousand Dollar Club.

The Thousand Dollar Club

Every woodworking student wanted to be a member of the exclusive Thousand Dollar Club, but only a select few ever made it. It goes without saying that hard work was a prerequisite to gaining membership. Students earned $15 for each product sold, so to earn a paycheck of a thousand dollars or more, students had to sell at least sixty-seven products. Believe me, that's not an easy task for a shy self-conscious teenager!

This group never took the easy way — they did it the old-fashioned way, with hard work. This exclusive club consisted of: Colton Conrad, Chelsey Herod, Kristin McAlexander, Jerod Reeves, Nate Browning, John Bauer, Madison Aaberg, Guy Fortney, Tanya Letamendi, and Amanda Cramer.

Amanda Cramer holds the all-time sales record. She sold eighty-eight chairs and earned $1,320. She took $600 and treated her mother to a spa day at the exclusive Broadmoor Hotel in Colorado Springs.

When I asked, "Where's *my* spa day?" Amanda giggled. The next day she gave me a gift bag filled with a nail file, lotions, and soap.

"Have a great spa day," she said, while laughing her head off the whole time. Kids!

Doughnut Derby

Once all of the mass-production projects are completely assembled and constructed, they need to be sanded. In a typical year, that's anywhere between 350 to 500 projects. This is an enormous task. I enlist all of my classes to help out, with doughnuts as the bribe.

"The class that sands the most projects wins 100 doughnuts," I usually tell the classes several days before, just to build excitement.

On the day of the contest I'm yelling, "When the Doughnut Derby comes to town, everybody be jumpin' 'round!" The kids are usually all fired up!

Then I tell them, "The class that wins gets 100 doughnuts, plus the chance to compete in the Doughnut Derby."

"What's that?" each class asks.

"You get to pick two classmates who can eat twenty dough-nuts together. If they do it, I'll buy the class pizza."

Now the classes are ecstatic! They literally run out into the shop and sand for days! It's actually kind of hilarious to watch kids bustin' their hump for a box of doughnuts.

The year Aaron Sanchez's class won, his two classmates couldn't finish the twenty doughnuts. It's no wonder; these were special doughnuts. They were very large cinnamon rolls that I drilled holes in the center using the drill press. Everyone was laughing!

Aaron ate about ten regular doughnuts while he watched his two classmates fail to complete the doughnut derby. There were still eight of the special doughnuts left. Aaron wanted to win pizza for his class the next week.

"Mr. Conrad, if I finish eating those doughnuts, will you still buy us pizza next week?" Aaron asked.

This was a complete violation of Doughnut Derby rules! But that didn't really matter. I knew he couldn't eat them, especially after already eating ten.

"Oh, go ahead," I said as the class erupted in cheers for Aaron.

What happened next was unexplainable and unbelievable! Aaron methodically proceeded to consume the "special dough-nuts," almost as if he had a hollow leg. Just as time ran out, he stuffed the last one down.

"Time's up!" I screamed. "Open up."

Aaron dramatically opened his jaws, showing everyone he did it. The class went crazy. Aaron fell to the floor, totally stuffed.

The next class period I went to visit Aaron. I wanted to see how he was doing and play a joke on him. I picked a bunch of half-eaten doughnuts out of the trash can. I arranged them neatly in the same box Aaron had just eaten out of. When I got to Aaron's class, he was lying in the hallway, still stuffed from the Doughnut Derby.

"Here, Aaron, I brought you some doughnuts," I said.

It was more than he could bear. Aaron quickly ran to the bathroom! I later was told several of his classmates found the box of half-eaten doughnuts I had left behind.

"Hey, look — doughnuts," they said. They ate them all!

Aaron Sanchez not only led his class to victory in the Doughnut Derby, he also led his high school football team to victory as the starting quarterback. Although many people told him he would be too small to play college football, he made them eat those words, just like he did those doughnuts. Aaron is currently playing Division I football for the CSU Rams. With one year of eligibility left, I'm anxious to see how he chews up the competition next season. That's excellent!

Santa's Wood Shop

Every year, starting in November, my advanced woods class put their projects aside to build wooden toys for the children in our community. Then just before Christmas break, we transform the wood shop into the North Pole. My students dress up as elves, and we invite the whole town for the festivities. Santa and Mrs. Claus are present. The choir sings Christmas carols, the elves work on their toys, and we even let the little kids break open some piñatas filled with treats.

We call these "perky" three-to-five-year old kids up front to sit on Santa's lap, and that's when the elves present them with their wooden toys. My elves had made large wooden rocking horses, airplane scooters, and motorcycles.

The whole evening is incredible! Many parents are teary-eyed as they watch a teenager give their child a toy. I have to admit, I got a little choked up the first time I witnessed it. I remember thinking how cool it would be if one day these little kids would grow up and eventually take wood shop. Then they could make a toy to give away. Well, in 2003 it happened. One of my students made a rocking horse, just like the one he received at Santa's Wood Shop when he was six years old. Santa's Wood Shop has gone full circle.

None of this would have been possible without the help of Samuelson's Hardware. Mark Samuelson has donated hundreds of dollars worth of materials each year, enabling us to build all of those toys. Some former elves now work for Mark. Thanks, Mark, for helping perpetuate our Tradition of Excellence.

I obviously feel a great sense of pride and accomplishment over this Tradition of Excellence. I am very proud of all my students. It's very rewarding to know I played a small role in their success. It's funny, really, to think that this Tradition of Excellence all started the day I ***refused to be average...***

The Unstoppable You challenges you to create your own Tradition of Excellence.

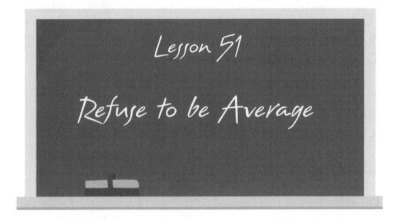

Lesson 51

Refuse to be Average

WARNING: If you follow the advice of this lesson, be prepared for the sling of arrows. These arrows can come from friends, family members, coworkers, and your superiors. I'm not going to tell you it doesn't hurt when one of those arrows hits you. It does. The good news is, other people's arrows can't stop you: *you* are the only one who can stop you. So refuse to be average and choose to be Unstoppable!

I got hit very early in my teaching career with one of those arrows. To this day, I still don't know who shot it. But I sure as heck know where it hit me...right in the rear end. The arrow, shot from behind, came in the form of an award I received anonymously. The award was called The A**hole of the Year. It was the *only* award I ever received from my school during my twenty-six years of teaching, and here's how I got it.

As I previously mentioned in Lesson 2, You're Fired, I lost my teaching job after my second year because another teacher had low enrollment. When I got my old job back, I vowed to never let that happen again. I inherited a part-time job with three classes of barely ten kids in each class. I employed several different tactics and worked endlessly to rebuild the program. Less than five years later, 175 kids signed up for my class, representing seven full classes. Initially, I thought everyone would be happy the Woods program was saved. What I didn't realize was that many of my co-workers were sharpening their arrows.

Having 175 kids sign up for wood shop caused two major problems. First, teachers only taught five classes a day, so I would have to be paid extra to teach two additional classes. That "extra" amounted to an additonal one-third of my salary. Second, with so many kids signed up for Woods, many other teachers had dramatic drops in their enrollment — so much so that several had to pick up classes outside their area of expertise just to have a full-time job. Instantly, I became the target, and the arrows started flying.

After all, as one teacher said, "Why should the wood shop teacher be paid more than the principal?"

I went before the school board to plead my case. "The reason so many kids want to take my class is because of the Friday Stories," I told the board.

They agreed to allow me to teach all of those classes. I would have to come to work an hour before school started just to teach the Zero Hour class, then teach the rest of the day without a break. None of this mattered to the rest of the faculty. Now they were taking shots at the school board, too!

Unfortunately, the school system is no different than many other work places. All the workers must "tow the line." No one must "dare to be different," because everyone must "fit the mold." "Striving to be average," I like to say.

In fact, in many ways, the school system is worse than other work places. You're paid not by how well you do your job, but by how long you've been there. Best of all, especially if you're average, once you've been there long enough, you can't even be fired!

The problem with some teachers isn't that they're burnt out. Their problem is that they were never lit to begin with! Well, believe me, the staff was lit now! They started shooting flaming arrows! The superintendent of the school district, Dr. Charles Grove, called an emergency meeting at the high school.

Dr. Grove tried to convince the staff to put away their weapons and call a cease-fire. It didn't work. They started shooting in *his* direction. It quickly became chaotic, with arrows flying everywhere. The whole time, I didn't say a word: I knew I was the reason we were there. I kept telling myself, "Shut up, shut up," as I ducked from the flaming arrrows.

It wasn't until after the teachers union at that time started spewing their "striving to be average" doctrine that I'd had enough. I spoke my mind. I had everyone's undivided attention, and not everyone liked what I was saying. The very next day, someone hung The A**hole of the Year award in the faculty lounge. Since I never went in the faculty lounge (still don't), the entire staff knew I was the recipient of the award before some coward stuck it in my mailbox.

While most "normal" teachers display their degrees and awards in their office, I only have one — The A**hole of the Year. It represents to me that I was the crab that got out of the bucket. It was a great feeling being out of the bucket, but that didn't mean the arrows ceased.

When I first started *The Unstoppable You* program, it drove some people crazy. They couldn't accept the fact that other schools and organizations would pay me to hear those Friday Stories. They tried everything in their power to stop it. They never succeeded. Which brings me to the point of this story...

If you're going to refuse to be average and dare to be different some people will try to stop you. Those envious people may be your friends, coworkers, family, or even your boss. I believe those people are there for a reason — to test your resolve. Basically, you have one of two choices: You can cave in, quit, and accept being Stoppable, or you can refuse to be average and choose to be Unstoppable! The choice is yours. But you were not created to be average!

Since receiving the A**hole of the Year award, I have spoken to well over 100 different schools and organizations in half a dozen states as of this writing — while still teaching full-time. I've also shaken the hands of close to 100,000 people who I've personally challenged to be Unstoppable. So I owe a tiny bit of gratitude to all of those arrow slingers: they were the fuel that kept my fires of desire burning.

My challenge to you is to take all of those negative forces in your life and throw them into your fire of burning desire. It will transform you into becoming a ***master of emotions...***

The cream that rises to the top is
The Unstoppable You.

Lesson 52

Master of Emotions

ZACH DREW MADE TWO RECURVE BOWS his senior year in Woods. Both bows were beautiful, but one was exceptional. That bow was unlike any that had ever been made before in my class. Zach made the riser (the part where you hold the bow) out of purple heart and white ash. What made this bow a work of art was the checkerboard pattern he incorporated into the design.

Zach spent countless hours shaping, filing, and sanding this beautiful work of art. The finish was flawless. Unfortunately, the first time Zach shot an arrow, the bow snapped in two, breaking apart across the checkerboard pattern.

When Zach walked into the shop that day and showed me what had just happened, I wanted to cry...literally. Zach, on the other hand, remained poised and relatively calm, considering what had just happened. He later attributed his self-control to a story I had read to his class over two years before. The title of the story was called Today I Will Be Master of My Emotions by Og Mandino.

Needless to say, I was impressed. First, because he recalled the story, and second, because he was living it. I remember wishing I could master my emotions as well as Zach did the next time adversity struck. I guess that's why people say, "Be careful what you wish for." The very next day, I would get my wish...and my test.

The following day, I demonstrated to Dee Brockman and her

class how to use the Keller Dovetail System. Dee needed to use this expensive system on her project. I spent considerable time instructing her and her class on its proper use. When I finished, I warned the class, "Be careful, this system is very costly and hard to replace."

I no sooner turned my back when tragedy struck. The clamp fell off Dee's workpiece. This caused the router bit to shatter and sent the Keller Dovetail System crashing to the cement floor. It all happened in an instant and made a horrific sound. Dee was in tears, and I could see that every eye in the shop was on me, waiting to see what I was going to do. Several other students needed to use this same exact setup; now it was toast. I wanted to scream! I felt myself getting ready to lose it.

Then suddenly, from out of nowhere, I thought about Zach. So, I turned and walked into my office. I sat down and repeated the words out loud, "The kid is more important than the tool," at least ten times.

After I calmed down, I walked back into the shop to console Dee. She was still sobbing. I put my hand on her shoulder and told her it was going to be all right, but she needed to order another bit right away. The last time I ordered a bit it took two weeks to get it.

Unbelievably, the next morning at eight o'clock, Dee's mom — Marianne — had the new bit in her hand. After hearing what had happened, she used her expertise from her job at our local ranch and home supply store to rush deliver another bit. But wait, it gets better!

Shortly after delivering the bit, Marianne returned with a huge yellow box. Inside was over $600 worth of battery-powered DeWalt tools. "Merry Christmas," she said.

"Wait a second," I said. "This is the month of May."

"This gift is a donation from Murdoch's Ranch and Home Supply. We just wanted to help you and your students," beamed Marianne.

Wow! I couldn't believe it! My classes sent Murdoch's a thank-you letter signed by all of the kids. They use those tools every day. Amazing things happen when you master your emotions. As for

Zach, he glued his bow back together and took Best of Show honors at our annual woodworking show. And as for Dee, I told her she could break anything she wanted to.

I believe God blesses those who master their emotions, but there also comes a time when you have to ***push back...***

Mastering emotion is key to creating
The Unstoppable You.

Lesson 53

Push Back

GLENN DUZIK WAS A BASKETBALL PLAYER. I met Glenn during my first year teaching. He was a tall, slender farm boy who loved basketball. He even had a hoop set up out on his family's ranch. The problem was he wasn't that good of a player. Although Glenn had many of the skills, he lacked the confidence needed to become a great player — or, for that matter, to even be a starter on his high school team.

Much of Glenn's lack of confidence was due in part to a comment his freshmen coach had made at the end of the season. While addressing his team, the coach told the players not to go around making excuses, or what he called "a loser's limp." Glenn interpreted that comment to mean he was a limping loser. Glenn was "lower than a snake's belly in a wagon rut" when his father, Duke, asked if I'd help his son become a better ball player. Duke discovered that I had played college basketball from our principal, Joe Janosec. Joe had told Duke about the new teacher he had just hired, and that he had an illustrious basketball background. So, that's how it came about that Glenn became my first project.

I really liked Glenn. He reminded me of myself at that age. There wasn't a mean or aggressive bone in his body, but I knew that would have to change. For starters, I showed Glenn my scrapbook, something I had never done before or, for that matter, since. I shared my low point, the day my coach asked me for my uniform so another kid could wear it. We didn't have enough to go around, so I sat on the bench that next game wearing a T-shirt. As Glenn turned page after page of the scrapbook, reading the articles and seeing the pictures of the high points from my glory days, I asked him, "How bad do you want it?"

A misty-eyed Glenn replied, "I want it more than anything."

I assured Glenn he could have that same success, but it was going to take a lot of hard work. The very next day, the hard work began.

My first rule was, "No more getting rides to school or practice." I made him ride his bike over ten miles a day. The second rule was weight lifting at least three times a week. But the third rule was the most important one of all: he had to play basketball against me every day after school. This was how I was going to transform Glenn into a lean, mean, basketball machine.

Day after day, we played ball. Sometimes it was just the two of us; other days there were enough guys to pick teams. Regardless of the number of players, one thing was always the same: Glenn and I guarded each other. We were *never* on the same team.

Looking back, those days in the gym could best be described as child abuse. I pushed and knocked Glenn around and down countless times. He was so happy I was "helping" him that he never complained. He would get back up, smile at me, dust himself off, and keep playing. This just made me push harder. I wanted him to push back. He never did. Day after day, week after week, month after month, Glenn would get back up, smile, and keep playing. I was starting to lose hope that he would ever become aggressive enough to push back. Then one day it happened...

I fouled Glenn hard one day. Actually, the foul was on the borderline of being a cheap shot. Glenn hit the floor hard, and some of his teammates ran over to see if he was all right. What happened next would be a defining moment in young Glenn's life. Instead of smiling, Glenn came right at me. He pushed me in the chest with both hands and yelled, "I'm sick of your !*?T!"

He wanted to fight. At long last, Glenn had had enough. I guess all those years of getting pushed around had bottled up inside of him. Now the cap blew off and emotion was flowing everywhere. I was so happy I wanted to hug him, but I couldn't blow my cover. I pushed him back. I yelled, "You want a piece of this? Let's go!"

I put up my fists. I was "talking smack," putting on a show. The whole time I was waiting for someone to step in and stop this nonsense. Luckily, the other players pulled us apart. Glenn was so upset he was in tears. I was supposed to be his friend...What Glenn didn't realize was he had just been transformed into a lean, mean, basketball machine. Mission accomplished!

As soon as I got home that day, I called his dad. "Duke," I said, "he's ready."

I proudly watched Glenn his senior year dominate the district semi-final game at Mesa State College in Grand Junction. He scored twenty-plus points, and had several blocked shots and a ton of rebounds. He had to guard a 6'8" kid from Grand Junction Central who was their leading scorer. Glenn played awesome and aggressive defense, shutting him down. Glenn and his team won the game — and the next night, they won the district championship.

Afterward, in front of everyone at the game, Glenn's mom — Jacque — hugged me. With tears of pride and joy streaming down her cheeks, she said, "That all happened because of you."

I thanked and corrected her. "That all happened because Glenn pushed back." Glenn had definitely passed *the man test...*

Sometimes *The Unstoppable You* must push back.

Lesson 54

The Man Test

IN THE SPRING OF 2007, two of my advanced woodworking students came late to my class. One of them was my son, Colton. For both of them, it was their second tardy. Everyone in the class celebrated knowing their punishment meant they had to attempt to do The Man Test.

The Man Test is a physical and mental test of will. It consists of a wall sit while holding a forty-five-pound weight straight out with your arms, while simultaneously repeating a complicated phrase twenty times, promising never to be late again. Of course, it's all done in front of the entire class. It's quality entertainment! Even the perpetrators get a kick out of it. Since both boys failed the complicated phrase portion of the test, they each had to do 100 push-ups. Everyone was in hysterics afterward. Little did any of us realize that less than fifteen minutes later, the *real* Man Test was about to unfold...

While working on a queen size bed he had designed, Billy Ivy called me over to ask a question. After I answered him, I glanced at him to verify he understood.

Billy nodded his head yes. That's when I noticed a lump sticking out from the side of his jaw.

"What's that?" I asked.

At first Billy said, "It's nothing."

Then I touched the lump with my finger and said, "No, what is that?"

I was concerned it was some kind of growth that might require medical attention. Seriously, I wasn't prepared for the answer when Billy told me, "It's chew."

I was shocked! Billy, the star pitcher for our playoff-bound baseball team, was chewing tobacco the day before the biggest game of his life. The school athletic policy on any tobacco or substance use is very clear: the athlete loses two weeks or two games of eligibility. This policy would effectively end Billy's senior year season if I turned him in.

I called Billy into my office. My first question was, "Why would you chew tobacco the day before the biggest game of your life? Especially in my class?"

Billy's response was, "I don't know — just being stupid, I guess."

I requested Billy spit the chew out and give me the tin with the rest of the tobacco. Without hesitation, Billy did just that. I told him I wasn't sure what I was going to do. I was a bit angry and confused. I was angry at Billy for putting both of us in this situation and confused as to what to do about it. Turning him in would put a certain end to his high school baseball career. Not turning him in would be a violation of state law, school policy, and a city ordinance, and there would be certain disciplinary action against me from the high school administration. Most of all, I worried about the message I would be sending Billy about my own character and integrity if I didn't turn him in. After all, I am the guy who travels around the country speaking to kids with *The Unstoppable You* program. I needed time to think. I sent Billy back into the shop to work on his project.

Immediately I tried to call Billy's parents, Preston and Cheryl Ivy. But they weren't at home, because they had already left. I knew where they were headed, since my wife, Vicki, was traveling with them. The three of them were going to watch the Ivy's other son, Brian, and my son, Colton, at a track meet in Grand Junction later that day. From there, the Ivys would drive to Denver to watch Billy pitch the next day in the first game of the baseball playoffs. This situation only compounded my dilemma about what to do. The Ivys were (and still are) our friends. To top it off, the baseball team would be leaving school in less than forty minutes. I had to act now. I called Billy back into my office. He sat down on the couch.

Since most of my teaching I do with the use of stories and their lessons, I shared two stories with Billy. Both were about two other kids who sat on the exact same couch.

The first story was about a kid who, twenty years ago, was the captain of his team. Several of his teammates were caught and later confessed to using tobacco in their motel room during an away game. Their punishment was that they had to miss the next two weeks of practice and games. Although this captain was never questioned, he admitted to me he had used tobacco, too. I told this captain he needed to step up as the leader of the team and take his punishment like the others. I told him that not doing so would split his team apart and cause animosity with those who had confessed. In addition, I told him his team would definitely lose without him, but they would be a stronger team in the long run.

"This isn't about the win/loss record," I said. "This is about being a man."

At that point, this captain asked if he could be excused so he could go talk to his coach. I sincerely believed he was going to turn himself in. However, after our meeting, he never missed a game. I never really found out what happened that day after he left the couch. I do know this captain and his team had a miserable season after that. The coach eventually resigned under extreme parental pressure. Integrity issues were the parent's biggest concern.

The second story I shared with Billy was about Clint Haskins. "Clint sat on the same couch as you, Billy, when he told me he was going to plead guilty to drinking and driving the night his truck collided with a Jeep Wagoneer. All eight passengers in the Jeep were killed. Clint's punishment wasn't missing a few games," I told Billy. "It was twenty years in prison. Clint lost quite a few years of freedom, but he kept his integrity by accepting responsibility for his actions."

Billy sat there nodding his head so I knew he had gotten the point. I asked him if he had ever chewed tobacco in my class before.

"Yes, on several occasions," Billy admitted.

"Yet I never noticed it before," I said. "I believe God wanted me to catch you today, the worst possible day for you," I told Billy. "Maybe it's because you're going to get cancer from chewing, or maybe it's going to cause you other problems. I really don't know why, Billy, but I honestly believe God wanted me to catch you today."

"What would your dad do if he were me in this situation?" I asked Billy.

"He'd turn me in."

"I already know what your mom would do."

Billy agreed, "She'd turn me in, too."

Billy even talked about his grandfather and said he would do the same. It was obvious Billy had tons of respect for the integrity of his parents and grandfather. At that point, I handed Billy his can of chew.

"Well, Billy, since you caused this problem, I'm leaving it up to you to solve it."

I shook his hand and walked out of my office. Billy sat there momentarily, then made one of the biggest decisions I had ever seen from a kid. He got up off the couch and walked into the athletic director's office, knowing full well what the ramifications were going to be. Billy turned himself in.

What Billy lost that day paled in comparison to what he gained. You see, "Billy the Kid" became "Billy the Man" that day. He definitely passed The Man Test! The thing that impressed me most about Billy was he never once before, during, or after the incident ***complained of sore feet...***

If given The Man Test, what grade would *you* receive? *The Unstoppable You* passes with flying colors!

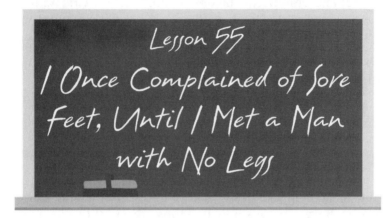

Lesson 55
I Once Complained of Sore Feet, Until I Met a Man with No Legs

THE TITLE OF THIS STORY SAYS IT ALL. No matter how bad your situation is, someone else has it worse. If a person with no legs can become Unstoppable, a person with sore feet has little to complain about. Several years ago, one of my students started complaining of "sore feet," so that Friday I introduced him to "a man with no legs."

This student with "sore feet" was complaining that he wasn't going to finish his woods project. With only two weeks of school left, he had developed a laundry list of excuses why he would be unable to complete it.

He finished his "sore feet" tirade by saying, "And there's nothing you can do about it."

All of my students know they must finish their projects to pass the class, and Mr. Sore Feet knew this as well. He was a senior and had taken my class for four years. This wasn't the first time he'd complained of sore feet, but I was determined to make it the last time. I didn't say a word to Mr. Sore Feet that day. I would have someone else do my talking.

All week long, I made phone calls and preparations for what would become not only my favorite Friday Story, but one of the most famous as well. The Associated Press picked up the story in newspapers nationwide.

All of my shop students were dismissed from their regular classes that Friday morning to attend the final Friday Story of the year. Well over 100 kids jammed into my classroom, they packed in like sardines. Not one of them had a clue of what was about to take place. On the table in front of the classroom I had a speaker-phone and my stereo.

Once they were settled, without saying a word, I smiled at them and walked over to the stereo. The drama was just beginning. I turn on the record player (old school). I slowly lowered the needle. Bob Dylan started to sing the song, "The Times They Are A Changin.'"

"Come gather 'round people wherever you roam and admit that the waters around you have grown and accept it that soon you'll be drenched to the bone. If your time to you is worth savin', then you better start swimmin' or you'll sink like a stone for the times they are a-changin.'"

When I lifted the needle off the record, there was complete silence in the room. Some of the students were trying to anticipate what I was going to say, others were confused. But they were all *thinking*. I loved it!

"Mr. Dylan is singing about change," I said forcefully while pointing to the seniors in my room. "Because the one constant I can guarantee all of you when you leave high school is that things will change. How you handle that change will play a huge role in how successful you become. Some change you will bring about yourself...college, marriage, jobs. Hopefully, those will be good and positive changes. But then there's going to be change that just *happens* to you. No way in a million years would you want this change."

Then I boldly sang as loud as I could, "And now you better start swimming or you'll sink like a stone, for the times they are a changing!"

My kids were spellbound as I walked over and picked up the phone. As I dialed the number, I said, "The person who's going to speak to you today could have sunk like a stone."

As the ringing of the number came through the speaker-phone, the air was thick with anticipation. The voice of Julene

McCallister sliced through that thick air like a hot knife when she said, "Hello?"

After introducing Julene to my class, I asked her to tell what happened on that fateful day...

Julene started very strong, but it quickly became obvious she was crying. Her voice cracked with emotion as she talked about her son, Kacey. Her sobbing was uncontrollable as she described what she had witnessed.

She told the class how she watched her six-year-old son, Kacey, get run over by a tractor-trailer truck. After that, she couldn't even talk anymore. The only sound coming through the speakerphone was her weeping. It was intensely emotional. Over 100 kids were in shock, many of them crying, too.

It took a minute or so for Julene to compose herself. Then she described the horrific sight of watching her son being swept up in the big rig's swirling wheels.

"I remember the blood curdling screams," said Julene. "One leg was severed above the hip, the other six inches below it. As Kacey lay there bleeding to death, I gave him a kiss goodbye," a weeping Julene cried.

Kacey was rushed to a hospital and then to a rural airport, where he was flown through a blizzard in a small aircraft to the Salt Lake City Airport, where a helicopter took him to Children's Primary Hospital. Kacey was expected to die along the way. When he arrived at the hospital, Julene was still by his side.

"Now he was in the hands of God and the surgeons," Julene told my class.

Feeling helpless at that point, she did the only thing she could do — she prayed. Julene prayed harder than she ever had. She was praying for her son's life.

God answered Julene's prayers, I believe, so Kacey could be an inspiration to others. Now he was about to inspire my students — especially the one who complained about "sore feet."

As soon as Kacey started to talk, it was obvious he was only eleven years old. He had the voice of a child, but what he was about to say was anything but childish. I held a newspaper clipping high in the air with a picture of Kacey playing baseball. My students gasped when they saw it. Kacey's body seemed to be growing right out of the grass. The photograph looked surreal.

"Kacey," I said, "when I saw this picture of you in the newspaper, I knew you had to talk to my classes." I then shot a series of questions to Kacey, which he answered:

Q. Kacey, what time did you get up this morning?

Kacey. I get up every morning at 5:00 a.m.

Q. Why does a kid with no legs get up that early everyday?

Kacey. I have a newspaper route and I have to deliver the newspapers before school starts.

Q. How does a kid with no legs deliver newspapers?

Kacey. I usually use my wheelchair. (I held up a picture of Kacey delivering newspapers in his wheelchair.)

Q. Kacey, I read in this newspaper article that you went on a ten-mile tricycle trip. How does a kid with no legs peddle a bike?

Kacey. I have a custom-made bike I peddle with my arms. (I held up the picture of Kacey riding his bike.)

Q. I also read in this article that you play basketball. How does a kid with no legs run up and down the court?

Kacey. I just use my arms as my legs. (I held up the picture of Kacey playing basketball.)

Q. Kacey, I understand that you can swim. How does a kid with no legs swim? Do you wear a life jacket?

Kacey. No, life jackets are for people who can't swim.

Q. Kacey, how tall are you?

Kacey. I'm 2'7". The nice part about being so short is I get to sleep with all my stuffed toys. (I held up a picture of Kacey in bed with a mound of stuffed toys piled high while measuring the table that the phone was on. The table was exactly 2'7".)

Q. Kacey, I played a lot of basketball in my day, and if I'm ever picking teams, I'm picking you first — 'cause it's not about your physical height, it's all about your mental height! To me Kacey, you're a seven footer! Kacey, I have students who make excuses all the time about their problems. What advice would you give to those people?

Kacey. I realized there's nothing I can do to change my situation unless they come out with something that can grow legs. I just go with what I have.

After thanking Kacey and Julene, I hung up the phone. I told my kids, "Kacey would gladly take on all of your problems added up together just to be able to walk out of this classroom. Please don't complain to me about your sore feet, because you just met a man with no legs."

"One of the unsung heroes of this story is Kacey's mom, Julene," I told my classes. "Here's a mother who gave birth to her son, and later watched in horror as he was run over by a trac-tor-trailer truck. Immediately after the accident this same mother held her son and gave him what she thought would be her final kiss goodbye. Julene seldom left Kacey's side after this tragedy, praying to God the entire time. Then one day, through the grace of God, she brought Kacey home. While at home Kacey asked his mom to get him something to drink. And you know what your mom tells you when you ask her to go get you something you could easily get yourself. If she's like my mom she tells you, 'You got two legs, get it yourself.' But, what do you say to your son when he *doesn't* have two legs? What do you say then? This brave and loving mother, Julene, told Kacey to get it himself. Because she knew if she got Kacey that first drink, she'd be getting Kacey drinks for the rest of his life... Julene helped Kacey become Unstoppable!"

At that point, the student who said he wasn't going to get his project done stood up in front of 100 of his friends and classmates. He walked up to me. He was in tears. So were many others.

Mr. Sore Feet said, "Thank you, Mr. Conrad. I will never for-get this. Oh — by the way — I *will* finish my project."

Several days later, he completed his project.

I've shared this story with thousands of others. I also include video footage of Kacey wrestling one of my former students.

Kacey ends up winning the match 6-4. The reaction of the crowd is always the same. They are inspired to tears.

In the Fall of 2006, I spoke at a high school in Colorado. Afterward, a girl in a wheelchair introduced herself to me. Only months before she was in a motorcycle accident. She pulled her pant leg up and showed me her badly mangled leg.

"The surgeon who operated on my leg said I wouldn't be able to walk for six years," she said. "Mr. Conrad, after seeing and hearing that story about Kacey, I'm going to be walking before prom!"

I made her promise to let me know when she was walking again. Less than three months later, she emailed me. I couldn't believe what I was reading.

"I'm proud to say I've proven the surgeons wrong. Seven months since the accident, I'm walking all on my own!"

This girl got some of her inspiration from hearing the story about Kacey and Julene, who showed the world what's possible with **puppy love...**

The Unstoppable You doesn't complain of sore feet.

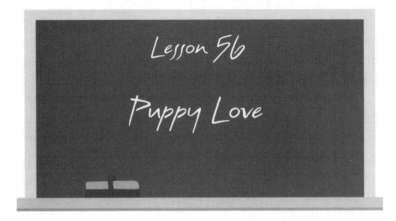

Lesson 56

Puppy Love

ONE OF LIFE'S BEST LESSONS can be learned from a puppy dog. Their unconditional love is a quality more of us should emulate. No matter how bad a day you've had, or how mad or upset you feel, your dog is always glad to see you. He greets you by jumping in the air, wagging his tail, and — quite possibly — licking you to death.

Now, I'm not suggesting we go around jumping in the air and licking each other, but I gotta think this world would be a whole lot better place if we all had that unconditional puppy love for one another.

I felt that puppy love for my grandfather, Henry DeTurk. "Hank," as he was called by those closest to him, lived in a tiny home. A house painter by trade, he never earned much over minimum wage. He never owned a brand new car. He and my grandmother, Helen, reared three kids in that tiny home, which, for a long time, had no inside toilet. The fact that Pop Pop didn't have a lot of money never mattered to me. Besides, Pop Pop took me fishing ever since I was old enough to walk. He would always make time for that. Every time we fished together, no matter how good or bad the fishing was, he would always talk about someday going to Canada.

"I hear you catch a fish with every cast," I heard him say a million times.

It always made me feel a little bad, because I knew he would never be able to afford such a trip. I'll never forget how he reacted when I told him I had gotten a teaching job in Colorado. Although he was happy for me, I could sense he was sad, too. He was losing his fishing partner, and I was losing mine. Before I left Pennsylvania, we agreed to go fishing together one last time. We were going to fish for muskies, the fish of ten thousand casts.

On the day of our last fishing trip, we used big expensive lures to try and catch the elusive muskie. Every time Pop Pop's lure got stuck on a rock, I would strip down to my shorts and go diving down into the water, following his fishing line until I freed the lure. He never liked when I did it, but he sure liked getting his $9 lure back.

After several hours of casting, we didn't even get a single bite. I told Pop Pop I was going to try one more cast and then we would leave. He reluctantly agreed, all the while knowing it was going to be our last time fishing together. As I cast my line on that proverbial last cast, I never imagined what would happen next. Suddenly my lure stopped, just as if it had gotten snagged on a large rock. I set the hook out of frustration, thinking I would soon be swimming for my lure. That was when I noticed the line peeling out of my reel. This "rock" was swimming away from me! I yelled to Pop Pop. He ran a quarter of a mile back to my car to get the brand new telescoping fishnet he had proudly purchased. It still had the price tag on it as he lowered it into the water.

Together, we eventually landed a fifty-inch muskie that weighed close to thirty pounds, but only after it snapped the telescoping handle right off the brand new net. Neither of us cared about that as we were dancing and jumping around, celebrating like two little kids. That fish ended up being the largest ever caught in Berks County at that time. I got that "memory" mounted, and we even had our picture in the *Reading Times* newspaper — the two of us, forever captured in time, holding our final trophy fish. On the way home, Pop Pop mentioned something about fishing in Canada again. I made a vow to myself to somehow see that Pop Pop would get to live his dream, because he had just helped me live mine.

Well, several years later, after buying and renovating some property in Colorado, I was able to save up a few extra dollars. At that time, Pop Pop was working as a security officer at Albright College in Reading, Pennsylvania, when late one night, one of the dormitories caught fire. Pop Pop single-handedly got all of the students safely out of the burning building. He was later rushed to the hospital to be treated for smoke inhalation. Well-wishers sent him flowers and fruit baskets to show their gratitude for all the lives he saved. Henry "Hank" DeTurk was a hero. I knew what I had to do...

I called him on the phone to congratulate him. Then I asked him if he remembered how he always talked about someday going to Canada.

"Why, of course," he replied.

"Well, Pop Pop, I'd like to take you there, my treat for all of the times you took me fishing," I said. At first, there was just silence on the other end of the line. "Pop Pop, you still there?" I asked. When he finally answered, I could tell he'd been crying.

"Pack your stuff, buddy. You're going to Canada," I told him.

That summer, I took my dad and Pop Pop way up north, close to the Arctic Circle, for the fishing trip of a lifetime. We even flew in a float plane that landed right on the lake. I never witnessed my grandfather having so much fun, He was like a little kid again, and we caught hundreds of fish.

At one point, Pop Pop turned to me and said, "It's just like they said it was — a fish every cast."

I got that whole trip on video. It was a dream come true. Pop Pop had such a good time that when he got home, he was making plans to sell that tiny house he lived in and move out to Colorado. He was going to live in the apartment right next to our house until we could build him a log home on the property. Since NaNa had passed away years earlier, he could begin a new life. We could fish together whenever we wanted.

He was on his way home, after having his trip mapped out from the American Automobile Association, when he experienced a gall bladder attack. The pain was so excruciating that he had to stop his car on the roadside The operation he underwent resulted in a blood clot that unexpectedly went to his heart. Less than three months after our once in a lifetime trip, my fishing buddy was gone, forever.

After the funeral, all of the family sat and watched the video of Pop Pop and the fishing trip to Canada. We all laughed and cried as we watched him relive his dream. I am so thankful I took that video camera. For that, I said, ***"Thank God..."***

The Unstoppable You loves their puppies because they don't live forever.

Lesson 57

Thank God

Author's note: At the request of this individual, only his first name is used.

AS TEACHERS AND PARENTS, we give and give to our kids, never asking or expecting anything in return. However, if you don't make light of your responsibilities, your blessings will be many.

My son Colton first met Ned when they worked together one summer. I was introduced to him for the first time when I was asked to take Ned to the airport. Along the way, Ned told me how impressed he was with Colton. He talked about Colton's knowledge, character, and maturity level, considering his age. While thanking him, I quickly passed much of the credit on to his mother. She put her life on hold for two years to homeschool Colton when he was about to fall through the cracks at the public school he was attending.

As we drove that morning, Ned started asking me questions about what I do. Much of it he had already heard from Colton, but he started asking me specifics. I told Ned how I was a teacher for many years, and during that time, I started telling my students stories every Friday. These Friday Stories had become the source of material for my speaking engagements and a book I was writing. Showing even more interest, Ned asked what I spoke about.

Rather than try to explain, I simply told him that I tell stories, and each story has a valuable lesson.

I passed the time sharing some of those stories with Ned. I began with When It's Darkest, That's When the Stars Come Out. When I finished, I could see he was quite moved by the story, and he asked to hear another one. Since we had plenty of time, I told him the Fill Your Cup story. Ned did more than just listen, he was taking the stories to heart. He was reacting much the same way audiences do when they hear those stories for the first time at *The Unstoppable You* presentations. For a time, I felt like I was giving a "live" presentation to a crowd of one. What I never would have guessed was that this crowd of one was perhaps the most important I would ever speak to; most assuredly, it was the smallest.

After sharing a few more stories, we stopped at a local store. Ned needed to pick up a few items but said, "I want to talk with you when I get back."

Up until this point, I had been doing most of the talking, so I looked forward to hearing what Ned had to say. I could never have imagined what he said to me when he got back in the car. It was proof positive that God works in mysterious ways...

It was a good thing I had my seat belt on that day, or I might have fallen over. Ned went on to explain in the most humble and genuine way that he not only believed in what I was trying to do with *The Unstoppable You*, but that he wanted to help me accomplish those goals. Now I was the one getting emotional. After all those years struggling to get *The Unstoppable You* program out there, Ned made me an offer I couldn't refuse. In return, he wanted nothing for himself, except to remain anonymous.

When he reached his destination, his ride had failed to show up...thank God. At that moment, Ned took out his pen and a piece of yellow paper. He wrote down all of the ways he was willing to help. After he was finished, his ride showed up and he shook my hand and left.

To the people who passed me on the way home that day, I must have seemed like I had lost my mind. I was yelling and screaming joyfully to myself and crying the whole time. While reading that piece of yellow paper, I thought about all of the things that seemed so coincidental that led to that day. Some of those events happened years ago — like homeschooling Colton, which led to the development of his character that so impressed Ned — yet they were all destined to lead to what had transpired that day.

I thanked God like never before. I also realized that I was going to be expanding my lessons far beyond my classroom walls and was going to be making some major decisions. One of those decisions would be to *finish strong...*

The Unstoppable You remembers to thank God.

IT WAS VERY DIFFICULT TO BRIDLE MY ENTHUSIASM as I considered the possibilities that would lie ahead during my last year of teaching. With all the years of hard work invested, I never looked at it as retirement, but rather the opportunity to expand the walls of my classroom. Still, it was somewhat of a struggle between the existing responsibilities of my teaching job, and the new doors of opportunity that were opening up.

In trying to juggle so many things at once, including the writing of this book, at one point I considered putting an end to some of the things we did for so many years in the wood shop. These things had become traditions, even though they caused me a lot of extra time, work, and energy. I was trying to think of a socially acceptable way to put some of these traditions to rest when my son, Colton, told me to finish strong.

Now in his senior year, Colton didn't want me to give up on the very traditions he was now a part of. It was the exact advice I had given him years earlier! Funny, I didn't even think he was listening. With my words thrown back at me, I decided to keep all of the traditions and make the last year the best ever.

After all, I'm the one who for twenty-six years told my students, "If you're going to be great anywhere, you first have to grow where you are planted."

Twenty-three years ago, after getting RIFed, I told my wife I would leave my teaching job when I was ready, on my own terms. Well, my friends, the time has come...

Anyone can start anything, but
The Unstoppable You finishes strong!

THE STICKERS

The teacher who sponsored our S.T.A.N.D. group (students taking a new direction) stepped down in 1995. No other teachers were interested in taking over this anti-drug and alcohol sponsorship, so I volunteered. I was having great success with this message in my classroom on Fridays and figured it was time to spread the word. Since I wanted the message to literally "stick" around, I enlisted the artistic ability of one of my former students who had his own business, Garcia Graphics. Together, we created the UNSTOPPABLE stickers.

Everyone who makes the commitment to be UNSTOPPABLE gets their very own personal power sticker at the conclusion of *The Unstoppable You* program. This six-inch diameter sticker with it's strong graphic message in silver and black was designed to continue to reinforce and remind students to be UNSTOPPABLE. The clenched fist represents "The Power Within" to make your own positive choices and not be influenced by negative peer pressure.

Years later, I modified the message creating a second design because of the large number of adult groups and leadership conferences I was speaking to. Since its inception, I've handed out nearly one hundred thousand stickers to kids of all ages, college students, teachers, administrators, and business professionals.

See and read for yourself the success stories of those that chose to be UNSTOPPABLE at: www.theunstoppableyou.com or www. craigconrad.com

UNSTOPPABLE SCHOOLS

Don't miss the bus! Make your school the next stop for *The Unstoppable You* program.

Allow Craig Conrad to customize a phenomenal and dynamic Unstoppable You presentation specifically designed for *your* school, addressing *your* concerns, featuring big screen images of *your* students and staff, along with images and "live" footage from the stories you have just read. By combining humor and audience interaction, Craig will energize *your* school's program to be unforgettable and Unstoppable!

Testimonials

It is without reservation that I recommend Craig Conrad's The Unstoppable You *presentation. It was not only captivating to all who attended, but his message was truly motivating.*

Principal — East Detroit High School, Detroit, Michigan

I am proud to say I will be Unstoppable with goals, family, and drugs. Thank you for changing my life.

Student — Mitchell Public School, Mitchell, Nebraska

Craig Conrad's, The Unstoppable You, *was the most emotional influence I've ever had.*

Student — Mesa State College Leadership Conference

The true test of any program is the lasting impact. It has now been almost four months since the first program and I am continually hearing about "unstoppable" parties. Craig Conrad's message of "Being Unstoppable" is being lived. Students are having parties and labeling them "unstoppable" indicating that drugs, alcohol, putdowns, etc. are not acceptable at this activity. The students seemed determined to continue this pattern and I see more and more "I Am Unstoppable" stickers. As a school administrator, I could not be more pleased with the impact of Craig Conrad's assemblies. He is driving home the right message; it is our job as administrators, teachers, parents, and community members to maintain this momentum.

Superintendent of Schools — Rathdrum, Idaho